SHE DOES BUSINESS

Mastering Money Management for Women Entrepreneurs

Catherine Ledger

© Copyright (2024) Catherine Ledger

All rights reserved

SHE DOES BUSINESS: Mastering Money Management for Women Entrepreneurs

© Copyright (2024) All rights reserved.

Written by (Catherine Ledger)

Copyrights Notice

No part of this book may be reproduced in any form or by any electronic or mechanical means, including information storage and retrieval systems, without written permission from the author.

All rights reserved. Respective authors own all copyrights not held by the publisher.

All trademarks, service marks, product names, and the characteristics of any names mentioned in this book are considered the property of their respective owners and are used only for reference. No endorsement is implied when we use one of these terms.

Limited Liability - Disclaimer

Please note that the content of this book is based on personal experience and various information sources, and it is only for personal use.

Please note that the information contained within this document is for educational and entertainment purposes only and no warranties of any kind are declared or implied.

Readers acknowledge that the author is not engaging in the rendering of legal, financial or professional advice. Please consult a licensed professional before attempting any techniques outlined in this book.

Nothing in this book is intended to replace common sense or legal accounting, or professional advice and is meant only to inform.

Your circumstances may not be suited to the example illustrated in this book; in fact, they likely will not be.

You should use the information in this book at your own risk. The reader is responsible for his or her actions.

The information provided herein is stated to be truthful and consistent, in that any liability, in terms of inattention or otherwise, by any usage or abuse of any policies, processes, or directions contained within is the solitary and utter responsibility of the recipient reader.

By reading this book, the reader agrees that under no circumstances is the author responsible for any losses, direct or indirect, which are incurred because of the use of the information contained within this document, including, but not limited to, errors, omissions, or inaccuracies.

Table of contents

Introduction 17
   Why This Book? 17
   What You Will Learn 17
   How This Book Can Help You 19
Welcome to Your Financial Empowerment 20
CHAPTER 1 21
PART I: FOUNDATIONS OF FINANCIAL MASTERY 21
The Financial Basics Every Woman Should Know 22
   Understanding Money Management 22
   Essential Financial Terms 22
Understanding Money Management 23
   The Importance of Budgeting 23
   Saving: Building Your Financial Safety Net 24
   Spending Wisely: The Power of Intentionality 25
   Tracking and Adjusting: Staying on Top of Your Finances 26
Essential Financial Terms 26
   Assets 27
   Liabilities 27
   Net Worth 27
   Revenue vs. Profit 28
   Cash Flow 28
   Interest 28
   Equity 29
   Diversification 29

- Liquidity 29
- ROI (Return on Investment) 30
- CHAPTER 2 31
- Setting Financial Goals 32
  - The Importance of Financial Goals 32
  - Types of Financial Goals 32
  - SMART Goals: A Framework for Success 34
  - Aligning Personal and Business Goals 34
  - Reviewing and Adjusting Your Goals 35
- Short-term vs Long-term Goals 35
  - Short-term Goals: Immediate Priorities 36
  - Long-term Goals: The Big Picture 37
  - Balancing Short-term and Long-term Goals 37
- SMART Goals for Financial Success 39
  - Specific: Defining Clear Objectives 39
  - Measurable: Tracking Your Progress 39
  - Achievable: Setting Realistic Expectations 40
  - Relevant: Aligning with Your Broader Objectives 40
  - Time-bound: Creating a Sense of Urgency 41
  - Putting It All Together: The SMART Goal Formula 41
- CHAPTER 3 43
- Budgeting for Success 44
  - The Purpose of a Budget 44
  - Building Your Budget: A Step-by-Step Guide 45
  - Tools and Techniques for Effective Budget Management 46

Overcoming Common Budgeting Challenges 47
The Role of Budgeting in Financial Success 48
Creating a Winning Budget 49
Understanding Your Income Sources 49
Categorizing Expenses 49
Setting Priorities and Allocating Funds 50
Reviewing and Adjusting Your Budget 51
Staying Committed to Your Budget 52
Tools and Techniques for Effective Budget Management 53
Budgeting Software and Apps 53
The Envelope System 54
Zero-Based Budgeting 55
Automation for Consistency 56
Regular Budget Reviews 56
Combining Techniques for Maximum Effectiveness 57
CHAPTER 4 58
PART II: ADVANCED FINANCIAL MANAGEMENT 58
Saving and Investment Basics 59
The Importance of Saving 59
The Basics of Investing 60
Balancing Saving and Investing 61
Starting Small and Staying Consistent 62
The Long-Term Benefits of Saving and Investing 62
Why Saving Is Essential 63
Introduction to Investments 65

CHAPTER 5 68
Understanding and Obtaining Credit 69
Types of Credit Available 72
- Business Loans 72
- Lines of Credit 72
- Credit Cards 73
- Trade Credit 73
- Merchant Cash Advances 74
- Peer-to-Peer Lending 74
- SBA Loans 74

Building and Maintaining a Healthy Credit Score 75
- Understanding Your Credit Score 75
- Building a Strong Credit Score 76
- Maintaining a Healthy Credit Score 77
- The Long-Term Benefits of a Healthy Credit Score 78

CHAPTER 6 79
Debt Management Strategies 80
- Understanding Your Debt 80
- Prioritizing Debt Repayment 80
- Refinancing and Consolidation 81
- Creating a Repayment Plan 81
- Avoiding Future Debt Pitfalls 82
- The Psychological Aspect of Debt Management 83

How to Manage and Reduce Debt 84
- Assess Your Current Debt Situation 84

- Prioritize Your Debts 84
- Create a Repayment Plan 85
- Negotiate with Creditors 86
- Consider Consolidation or Refinancing................................... 86
- Cut Expenses and Increase Income 87
- Stay Committed and Monitor Progress 87
- Avoid Taking on New Debt 88

Negotiating with Creditors 89
- Assess Your Situation... 89
- Contact Your Creditors Early 89
- Know What You Want 90
- Be Prepared to Negotiate.. 90
- Get Everything in Writing 91
- Consider Professional Help... 91
- Follow Through and Stay Committed 91

CHAPTER 7 93

Navigating Funding Opportunities... 94
- Understanding Your Funding Needs.. 94
- Traditional Financing Options... 94
- Alternative Financing Options 95
- Preparing for the Funding Process 96
- Navigating the Challenges 97

Finding the Right Funding for Your Business 98
- Assess Your Business Needs 98
- Consider the Stage of Your Business 98

Evaluate the Cost of Capital 99
Align with Your Business Goals 99
Consider Flexibility and Control 100
Research and Compare Options 100
Grant and Loan Opportunities 102
Grants: Free Capital with a Competitive Edge 102
Loans: Flexible Financing with Clear Repayment Terms 103
Choosing Between Grants and Loans 105
CHAPTER 8 106
Part III: Financial Risks and Protection 106
Investment Strategies for Growth 107
Reinvesting in Your Business 107
Diversifying Your Investment Portfolio 108
Leveraging Compound Interest 108
Balancing Risk and Reward 109
Staying Informed and Adapting Your Strategy 110
Long-Term Perspective and Patience 110
Stocks, Bonds, and Mutual Funds 112
Stocks: Ownership with Growth Potential 112
Bonds: Stability and Income 113
Mutual Funds: Diversification Made Simple 113
Choosing the Right Mix for Your Portfolio 114
Real Estate and Other Investment Vehicles 116
Real Estate: Tangible Assets with Long-Term Value 116
Other Investment Vehicles: Exploring Alternative Opportunities
 117

    Balancing Traditional and Alternative Investments 118
CHAPTER 9 120
Risk Management 121
    Identifying Potential Risks 121
    Assessing the Impact 122
    Mitigating Risks 123
    Embracing Risk as Part of Growth 124
Identifying Financial Risks 125
    Cash Flow Risks 125
    Credit Risks 126
    Interest Rate Risks 126
    Market Risks 127
    Currency Risks 127
    Liquidity Risks 128
Mitigation Strategies 129
    Diversification 129
    Insurance 129
    Contingency Planning 130
    Hedging 131
    Strong Internal Controls 131
    Regular Risk Assessment and Review 132
CHAPTER 10 133
Insurance Essentials 134
    General Liability Insurance 134
    Professional Liability Insurance 134

- Property Insurance 135
- Business Interruption Insurance... 135
- Workers' Compensation Insurance 135
- Cyber Liability Insurance... 136
- Key Person Insurance 136
- Choosing the Right Coverage 137

Types of Insurance You Need 138
- General Liability Insurance 138
- Professional Liability Insurance 138
- Property Insurance 139
- Business Interruption Insurance... 139
- Workers' Compensation Insurance 139
- Cyber Liability Insurance... 139
- Key Person Insurance 140
- Commercial Auto Insurance 140
- Product Liability Insurance 140
- Directors and Officers (D&O) Insurance 141

Understanding Policies and Claims... 142
- Reading and Comprehending Your Insurance Policies 142
- The Claims Process 143
- Avoiding Common Pitfalls... 144

CHAPTER 11.. 146

Legal Considerations 147
- Business Structure.. 147
- Contracts and Agreements.. 148

- Intellectual Property Protection 149
- Employment Law 150
- Regulatory Compliance 151

Legal Structures for Business 152
- Sole Proprietorship 152
- Partnership 152
- Limited Liability Company (LLC) 153
- Corporation 153
- S Corporation 154
- Nonprofit Organization 154
- Choosing the Right Structure 155

Protecting Your Business Legally 156

CHAPTER 12 159

Part IV: Planning for the Future 159

Tax Planning and Benefits 159

Preparing for Tax Season 162

Maximizing Your Deductions 165

CHAPTER 13 168

Retirement Planning 169

Understanding Retirement Accounts 171

Planning for Financial Independence 173

CHAPTER 14 175

Succession Planning 176

Preparing Your Business for Transition 178

Estate Planning Basics 180

CHAPTER 15 183
Part V: Personal Growth and Financial Leadership 183
Developing a Financially Savvy Mindset 184
Overcoming Financial Fears 186
Building Confidence in Financial Decision Making 188
CHAPTER 16 191
Financial Negotiation Skills 192
Mastering Negotiation Techniques 194
Applying Negotiations to Financial Decisions 196
CHAPTER 17 199
The Future of Finance for Women Entrepreneurs 200
Trends and Opportunities 201
Staying Ahead in the Financial Game 203
Conclusion: Empowering Your Financial Journey 206

Introduction

Welcome to "She Does Business: Mastering Money Management for Women Entrepreneurs," a comprehensive guide designed to empower you, the ambitious woman entrepreneur, to take charge of your financial destiny. Authored by Catherine Ledger, this book is your gateway to becoming proficient in managing and maximizing your financial resources, which is foundational to both personal and business success.

In the following pages, you will discover a wealth of information tailored specifically to address the unique financial challenges and opportunities faced by women in business. From basic financial principles to advanced investment strategies, this book covers a broad spectrum of topics essential for every businesswoman's financial literacy and growth.

Why This Book?

In today's competitive world, financial acumen is a key driver of success. Yet, many women entrepreneurs find themselves at a disadvantage due to a lack of formal financial education or resources that speak directly to their needs. "She Does Business" is crafted to bridge this gap by providing you with practical, actionable knowledge that goes beyond traditional advice. Here, you'll learn not only how to manage money but also how to make it work effectively for you and your business.

What You Will Learn

- **Fundamentals of Personal and Business Finance:** Understand the building blocks of financial management, including budgeting, saving, and investing.

- **Strategic Planning for Financial Growth:** Learn how to set and achieve financial goals through clear, actionable strategies.
- **Navigating Funding and Investments:** Explore the avenues for raising capital, managing investments, and increasing your business's financial health.
- **Risk Management:** Gain insights on identifying potential financial risks and strategies to mitigate them effectively.
- **Legal and Tax Planning:** Equip yourself with knowledge about tax benefits, legal structures, and compliance to optimize your business operations and profitability.

How This Book Can Help You

Each chapter is designed to be both informative and practical, enabling you to implement what you've learned immediately. By the end of this book, you will have gained:

- **Increased Financial Literacy:** Deep understanding of financial terms and concepts that are crucial for running a business.
- **Confidence in Financial Decision-Making:** Ability to make informed decisions that positively impact your business and personal finances.
- **Strategic Financial Skills:** Skills to plan, execute, and manage your financial affairs with precision and foresight.

Whether you are just starting out or looking to enhance your financial skills, "She Does Business" is an invaluable resource that will guide you through the complexities of finance with clarity and confidence. This book is more than just a guide—it is your financial mentor in print.

Join Catherine Ledger in this empowering journey and transform the way you do business. Your path to financial mastery starts here.

Welcome to Your Financial Empowerment

CHAPTER 1

PART I: FOUNDATIONS OF FINANCIAL MASTERY

The Financial Basics Every Woman Should Know

Understanding the fundamentals of finance is the first step towards financial empowerment. As a woman entrepreneur, mastering these basics can provide you with the confidence and skills needed to make informed decisions that affect both your personal life and business ventures.

Understanding Money Management

Effective money management begins with understanding how to budget, save, and spend wisely. Budgeting involves creating a plan for your income and expenses, ensuring that you can cover your monthly obligations while setting aside funds for future goals. It's not just about restriction but about making smart choices that align with your financial objectives.

Learning to save is crucial. Savings can provide a safety net in times of unexpected expenses and are essential for long-term financial health. Start small, perhaps setting aside a fixed percentage of your income each month, and gradually increase as you become more comfortable with your budget.

Spending wisely means recognizing the difference between needs and wants. Prioritize expenditures that bring long-term benefits, such as investing in your business or purchasing health insurance, over more transient pleasures.

Essential Financial Terms

To confidently navigate the financial world, it's important to be fluent in its language. Here are some essential terms every woman entrepreneur should know:

Assets: Anything of value that you own that can be converted into cash. Examples include cash, investments, and property.

Liabilities: Any debts or financial obligations you owe. This includes loans, mortgages, and any other debts.

Net Worth: The difference between your assets and liabilities. Calculating your net worth gives you a clear picture of your current financial position.

Interest: The cost of borrowing money, typically expressed as a percentage of the principal loan amount.

Investment: The use of money with the expectation of achieving a higher return in the future. This can include purchasing stocks, bonds, or real estate.

By familiarizing yourself with these concepts, you can begin to take charge of your financial health, enabling you not just to manage but to grow your wealth effectively. As your understanding deepens, so will your ability to make strategic decisions that bolster both your personal and business finances.

Understanding Money Management

Money management is the cornerstone of financial success, both in your personal life and as an entrepreneur. It's not just about knowing how much money comes in and goes out—it's about making informed decisions that align with your goals, ensuring that your finances work for you, not against you. Understanding money management is essential for building a strong financial foundation that supports your business and personal aspirations.

The Importance of Budgeting

Budgeting is the process of creating a plan for your income and expenses. It's the first step in taking control of your finances. A well-crafted budget allows you to allocate funds towards your most important goals while ensuring that your daily needs are met. For entrepreneurs, this means having the resources to reinvest in your business, pay your employees, and maintain your personal financial health.

Start by categorizing your expenses into fixed and variable costs. Fixed costs include expenses that remain consistent each month, such as rent or mortgage payments, utilities, and insurance premiums. Variable costs fluctuate, such as groceries, entertainment, and business-related expenses like marketing or supplies. Tracking these costs helps you identify areas where you can reduce spending and reallocate funds towards more strategic investments.

A common approach to budgeting is the 50/30/20 rule: allocate 50% of your income to needs, 30% to wants, and 20% to savings and debt repayment. This simple framework helps ensure that you're not overspending in any one area and that you're consistently building a financial safety net.

Saving: Building Your Financial Safety Net

Saving is a critical component of money management. It's not just about putting money aside for a rainy day—it's about creating a financial cushion that can support you through unexpected challenges, whether in your personal life or your business. The COVID-19 pandemic, for example, highlighted the importance of having emergency savings to navigate sudden economic downturns.

Start by establishing an emergency fund that covers at least three to six months of living expenses. This fund should be easily accessible, like in a high-yield savings account, so you can quickly tap into it if needed. Beyond the emergency fund, consider setting aside savings for specific goals, such as purchasing new equipment for your business, funding a marketing campaign, or even taking a much-needed vacation.

The habit of saving regularly, even in small amounts, can make a significant impact over time. Automating your savings is an effective strategy—set up automatic transfers from your checking account to your savings account to ensure that saving becomes a non-negotiable part of your financial routine.

Spending Wisely: The Power of Intentionality

Spending wisely doesn't mean you have to deprive yourself of the things you enjoy. Rather, it's about making intentional decisions that align with your values and goals. For entrepreneurs, this means prioritizing investments that drive growth and sustainability in your business, while also taking care of your personal well-being.

Begin by distinguishing between needs and wants. Needs are essential expenses that are crucial for your daily life and the operation of your business—like rent, utilities, and inventory. Wants are non-essential, like dining out, luxury items, or unnecessary upgrades. While it's important to enjoy the fruits of your labor, making thoughtful decisions about where your money goes will help you build a stronger financial future.

Another key aspect of wise spending is avoiding lifestyle inflation. As your income increases, it can be tempting to upgrade your lifestyle accordingly. However, maintaining your current level of spending while your income grows can significantly boost your savings and investment potential, accelerating your progress toward financial independence.

Tracking and Adjusting: Staying on Top of Your Finances

Effective money management is not a set-it-and-forget-it process. It requires regular monitoring and adjustments to ensure that you stay on track with your financial goals. This involves reviewing your budget and spending patterns regularly, assessing your savings progress, and making changes as necessary.

There are numerous tools and apps available that can simplify this process, from basic spreadsheets to sophisticated financial planning software. Find a system that works for you and commit to reviewing your finances at least once a month. This will help you identify any issues early on and make informed decisions to keep your finances healthy.

Remember, money management is an ongoing journey. The more you engage with your finances, the more confident and empowered you will become in making financial decisions that support your business and your life. With these foundational skills, you are well on your way to mastering money management and achieving the financial success you deserve.

Essential Financial Terms

To navigate the world of finance confidently, it's crucial to understand the language of money. Financial terms might seem overwhelming at first, but once you grasp their meanings, you'll find that they are the keys to unlocking a deeper understanding of your financial situation and making informed decisions for your business and personal life. Below are some essential financial terms that every woman entrepreneur should know:

Assets

Assets are everything you own that has value and can be converted into cash. This includes both tangible items, like property and equipment, and intangible ones, like patents or trademarks. In a business context, assets can also include inventory, accounts receivable, and investments. Knowing what your assets are and understanding their value is crucial for assessing your financial health and leveraging these assets to secure loans or investments.

Liabilities

Liabilities are your financial obligations—what you owe to others. This includes debts, loans, mortgages, and other obligations such as unpaid bills or accounts payable. In a business setting, liabilities also encompass things like employee wages and taxes owed. Balancing your liabilities against your assets is key to maintaining a healthy financial status. The goal is to ensure that your liabilities are manageable and do not exceed your assets, which could put your business at risk.

Net Worth

Net worth is the difference between your assets and liabilities. It represents your overall financial standing and can be a positive or negative number. A positive net worth means you own more than you owe, while a negative net worth indicates that your liabilities exceed your assets. For entrepreneurs, understanding your net worth helps in assessing the value of your business and personal finances, and is crucial when seeking investments or loans.

Revenue vs. Profit

Revenue is the total amount of money your business earns from sales or services before any expenses are deducted. Profit, on the other hand, is what remains after all operating costs, taxes, and other expenses have been subtracted from your revenue. There are two types of profit: gross profit (revenue minus the cost of goods sold) and net profit (what remains after all expenses, including operating costs, taxes, and interest, are deducted). Understanding the difference between revenue and profit is essential for assessing the financial health of your business.

Cash Flow

Cash flow refers to the movement of money in and out of your business. Positive cash flow means more money is coming in than going out, which is crucial for covering expenses, paying employees, and reinvesting in your business. Negative cash flow, where expenses exceed income, can lead to financial difficulties. Monitoring and managing cash flow is critical for ensuring your business remains solvent and can continue to grow.

Interest

Interest is the cost of borrowing money, typically expressed as a percentage of the loan amount. It's what you pay on top of the principal when you take out a loan or use credit. Conversely, interest can also refer to the earnings you receive from investments, savings accounts, or bonds. Understanding interest rates and how they work can help you make informed decisions about borrowing, lending, and investing.

Equity

Equity represents the ownership value in your business, calculated by subtracting total liabilities from total assets. In a business context, equity can be divided among shareholders or retained entirely by the business owner. Building equity in your business increases its value and can be used as collateral for loans or to attract investors. For personal finances, equity often refers to the value of your ownership in a property, such as the equity in your home after accounting for the mortgage.

Diversification

Diversification is a risk management strategy that involves spreading your investments across various assets to reduce exposure to any one particular asset or risk. In business, diversification can also refer to expanding your product line or entering new markets to minimize the risk of relying on a single source of income. A well-diversified portfolio or business strategy can help you weather economic downturns and capitalize on opportunities in different areas.

Liquidity

Liquidity refers to how quickly and easily an asset can be converted into cash without significantly affecting its value. Cash is the most liquid asset, while real estate or equipment may take longer to sell and convert into cash, making them less liquid. For entrepreneurs, maintaining a certain level of liquidity is important to meet short-term obligations and take advantage of immediate opportunities.

ROI (Return on Investment)

ROI is a measure of the profitability of an investment, calculated by dividing the net profit from the investment by the initial cost of the investment, usually expressed as a percentage. Understanding ROI helps you evaluate the efficiency of your investments and make decisions that will maximize your returns. Whether you're investing in a new marketing campaign, buying new equipment, or considering a real estate purchase, calculating the ROI can guide you toward making the most profitable decisions.

By familiarizing yourself with these key financial terms, you'll be better equipped to manage your business finances with confidence and clarity. Understanding these concepts is not only crucial for day-to-day financial management but also for making strategic decisions that will shape the future of your business and personal wealth.

CHAPTER 2

Setting Financial Goals

Setting financial goals is one of the most powerful steps you can take on your journey to financial mastery. Clear, well-defined goals provide direction and motivation, enabling you to make decisions that align with your long-term vision. As a woman entrepreneur, your financial goals are not just about accumulating wealth—they are about creating a sustainable future for yourself, your business, and those who depend on you.

The Importance of Financial Goals

Financial goals are the foundation of a solid financial plan. They give purpose to your budgeting, saving, and investment activities. Without clear goals, it's easy to get sidetracked by day-to-day financial demands and lose sight of the bigger picture. Goals help you prioritize your spending, identify areas where you can cut back, and focus your efforts on what truly matters.

For entrepreneurs, financial goals can range from building an emergency fund, to growing your business, to planning for retirement. Each goal serves as a milestone that brings you closer to financial security and independence. By setting these goals, you create a roadmap that guides your financial decisions and helps you stay on track.

Types of Financial Goals

Financial goals generally fall into three categories: short-term, medium-term, and long-term. Understanding the differences between these can help you organize your priorities and develop a balanced financial strategy.

- **Short-Term Goals (0-1 year):** These are immediate priorities that you want to achieve within the next year. For example, saving for a specific piece of business equipment, paying off a credit card, or setting aside funds for a marketing campaign. Short-term goals require disciplined budgeting and consistent savings, but they are achievable within a relatively short time frame.

- **Medium-Term Goals (1-5 years):** These goals are slightly longer in duration and often involve larger sums of money. They might include expanding your business, saving for a significant personal investment like a home, or paying off a large portion of debt. Medium-term goals require a more strategic approach to saving and investing, as they often involve multiple steps to achieve.

- **Long-Term Goals (5+ years):** Long-term goals are your big-picture objectives, such as retirement planning, building a sizable investment portfolio, or planning for your children's education. These goals are typically the most challenging but also the most rewarding. They require a commitment to consistent saving and investment, as well as a clear understanding of your financial horizon.

SMART Goals: A Framework for Success

When setting financial goals, it's essential to make them SMART—Specific, Measurable, Achievable, Relevant, and Time-bound. This framework ensures that your goals are clear and actionable, making it easier to track your progress and stay motivated.

Specific: Be precise about what you want to achieve. Instead of saying, "I want to save money," specify the amount and purpose, such as "I want to save $10,000 for a business expansion."

Measurable: Ensure that your goal can be quantified so you can track your progress. For example, "I will save $500 a month for the next 20 months."

Achievable: Set goals that are challenging but realistic. Consider your current financial situation and determine what is feasible.

Relevant: Your goals should align with your broader life and business objectives. Ask yourself why this goal is important and how it fits into your overall financial plan.

Time-bound: Set a deadline for your goal. Having a clear timeline creates a sense of urgency and helps you stay focused.

Aligning Personal and Business Goals

As an entrepreneur, your personal and business finances are often intertwined. It's important to align your financial goals for both aspects of your life to avoid conflicts and ensure that one does not undermine the other. For instance, if your business goal is to expand into a new market, your personal goal might be to ensure you have the financial stability to support that growth.

Start by listing your top personal and business goals. Then, prioritize them based on urgency and impact. Look for areas where your goals overlap or where achieving one goal can help facilitate another. This integrated approach ensures that your financial goals are working together towards your overall success.

Reviewing and Adjusting Your Goals

Setting financial goals is not a one-time task—it's an ongoing process. As your life and business evolve, so too will your financial priorities. Regularly reviewing and adjusting your goals ensures that they remain relevant and attainable.

Schedule a quarterly or biannual review of your financial goals. During this time, assess your progress, celebrate milestones, and make any necessary adjustments. If you've achieved a goal ahead of schedule, consider setting a new one to keep pushing forward. If you're falling behind, analyze the reasons and adjust your strategy accordingly.

Remember, the purpose of setting financial goals is to create a clear path toward financial independence and success. By committing to this process, you're taking control of your financial future and empowering yourself to achieve your entrepreneurial dreams.

Short-term vs Long-term Goals

Setting financial goals is a crucial part of managing your money effectively, but not all goals are created equal. They can be broadly categorized into short-term and long-term goals, each serving a different purpose and requiring a different approach. Understanding the distinction between these two types of goals will help you prioritize your efforts and allocate your resources more efficiently.

Short-term Goals: Immediate Priorities

Short-term goals are objectives that you aim to achieve within a relatively short period, typically within one year. These goals often address immediate financial needs or opportunities and require focused, consistent effort to accomplish. For women entrepreneurs, short-term goals might include things like saving for a new piece of business equipment, paying off a small debt, or setting up an emergency fund.

Examples of short-term goals:

- **Saving $5,000 over the next six months** for a marketing campaign that could boost your business visibility and sales.

- **Paying off a high-interest credit card** within the next year to reduce financial stress and free up more cash flow.

- **Building an emergency fund** that covers three to six months of essential living and business expenses.

Short-term goals are essential because they provide immediate motivation and momentum. They are often more specific and measurable, making it easier to track your progress and stay committed. Achieving these goals can give you the confidence and financial stability needed to tackle more ambitious, long-term objectives.

Long-term Goals: The Big Picture

Long-term goals, on the other hand, are those that you plan to achieve over a longer horizon, typically five years or more. These goals are often more complex and require careful planning, sustained effort, and sometimes significant financial resources. Long-term goals for entrepreneurs might include expanding your business into new markets, building a diversified investment portfolio, or planning for retirement.

Examples of long-term goals:

- **Expanding your business nationally or internationally** within the next five to ten years, requiring substantial investment in infrastructure, marketing, and staffing.

- **Accumulating $1 million in retirement savings** over the next 20 years by contributing regularly to a retirement account and investing wisely.

- **Paying off your mortgage** within 15 years, freeing up significant cash flow for other investments or personal goals.

Long-term goals are the cornerstone of your overall financial strategy. They are often tied to your broader life and business vision, such as achieving financial independence, ensuring the longevity of your business, or securing a comfortable retirement. Because these goals are further out, they require patience, discipline, and regular reassessment to ensure you remain on track.

Balancing Short-term and Long-term Goals

While it's important to focus on both short-term and long-term goals, balancing them can be a challenge. Prioritizing one over the other might seem necessary at times, but it's essential to maintain a balance that ensures your immediate needs are met without compromising your future aspirations.

Here's how you can balance these goals:

- **Allocate resources wisely:** Set aside a portion of your income for short-term goals while also contributing consistently towards your long-term objectives. This could mean maintaining a savings account for immediate needs while regularly investing in a retirement fund.

- **Stay flexible:** Life and business are unpredictable, and your goals may need to adjust accordingly. If an opportunity arises that requires immediate attention, you might need to shift your focus temporarily. However, make sure you return to your long-term goals as soon as possible.

- **Regularly review your goals:** Conduct a quarterly or annual review of your financial goals. Assess your progress towards short-term goals and evaluate whether you're on track for your long-term aspirations. Adjust your strategies as needed to stay aligned with your overall financial plan.

By understanding and balancing short-term and long-term goals, you create a financial plan that not only addresses your current needs but also sets you up for future success. This dual approach ensures that you're making the most of your resources now while laying the groundwork for your dreams to become a reality down the road.

SMART Goals for Financial Success

Setting financial goals is a crucial part of achieving success, but how you set those goals can make all the difference. That's where the SMART framework comes in. SMART goals are Specific, Measurable, Achievable, Relevant, and Time-bound. This approach provides clarity, focus, and a clear path to success, ensuring that your financial goals are not just dreams but actionable plans.

Specific: Defining Clear Objectives

The first step in setting a SMART goal is to make it specific. A specific goal is clear and unambiguous, answering the fundamental questions: What do I want to accomplish? Why is this goal important? Who is involved? Where is it located? Which resources or constraints are involved?

For example, rather than setting a vague goal like "I want to save money," make it specific: "I want to save $10,000 over the next 12 months to fund a new marketing campaign for my business." This level of detail makes the goal concrete and gives you a clear target to aim for.

Measurable: Tracking Your Progress

A goal needs to be measurable so that you can track your progress and stay motivated. Measuring your progress helps you stay focused, meet deadlines, and feel the excitement of getting closer to achieving your goal. It answers the question: How much? How many? How will I know when it is accomplished?

Continuing with the previous example, if your goal is to save $10,000 in 12 months, you might break it down into smaller, measurable milestones, such as saving $833 per month. This way, you can regularly check in on your progress and adjust as necessary, ensuring you stay on track.

Achievable: Setting Realistic Expectations

While it's important to set ambitious goals, they must also be achievable. An achievable goal considers your financial situation, the constraints you may face, and the resources available to you. It answers the question: How can I accomplish this goal? Is this goal realistic given my current circumstances?

For instance, if your business is just starting out and you're dealing with limited cash flow, aiming to save $50,000 in a year might be unrealistic. Instead, a goal to save $10,000 might be more attainable, given your current income and expenses. The key is to stretch your abilities slightly, so the goal is challenging but not impossible.

Relevant: Aligning with Your Broader Objectives

A relevant goal matters to you and is aligned with other objectives you have set. Relevance ensures that the goal fits within the broader context of your personal and business life, answering the questions: Does this seem worthwhile? Is this the right time? Does this match our other efforts/needs?

For example, saving $10,000 is relevant if it directly supports a critical business objective, such as launching a new product or expanding your market reach. On the other hand, if your business is facing a different priority, such as paying down debt, then saving for a new campaign might not be as relevant at this time.

Time-bound: Creating a Sense of Urgency

Every goal needs a target date, something to work towards. Time-bound goals help you prioritize your tasks and focus your efforts, answering the questions: When? What can I do six months from now? What can I do six weeks from now? What can I do today?

Setting a deadline, like "save $10,000 in 12 months," creates a sense of urgency and helps you allocate time and resources appropriately. It also allows you to break the goal down into smaller, time-specific tasks, like monthly savings targets, making the overall goal more manageable.

Putting It All Together: The SMART Goal Formula

By ensuring your financial goals are Specific, Measurable, Achievable, Relevant, and Time-bound, you create a clear, actionable plan that is easier to follow and more likely to lead to success. Here's how a SMART goal might look in practice:

Specific: I want to save $10,000 to fund a new marketing campaign.

Measurable: I will save $833 each month for the next 12 months.

Achievable: Given my current business revenue and expenses, this savings goal is realistic.

Relevant: This goal aligns with my broader business objective of expanding my customer base.

Time-bound: I will achieve this goal by the end of the next 12 months.

Using the SMART framework, you transform vague aspirations into concrete plans, making it far more likely that you'll achieve your financial goals. Whether you're aiming to grow your business, increase your savings, or prepare for retirement, SMART goals provide the structure and clarity needed to turn your vision into reality.

CHAPTER 3

Budgeting for Success

Budgeting is the backbone of financial success, particularly for entrepreneurs navigating the complex world of business finance. A well-constructed budget provides a clear roadmap for where your money is going, helps you make informed decisions, and ensures that you are on track to meet your financial goals. In essence, budgeting is about controlling your finances, rather than letting them control you.

The Purpose of a Budget

At its core, a budget is a financial plan that outlines your expected income and expenses over a specific period, typically a month or a year. For entrepreneurs, budgeting serves multiple purposes:

Cash Flow Management: A budget helps you predict when money will come in and when it will go out, allowing you to ensure that you have enough cash on hand to cover your expenses and reinvest in your business.

Goal Setting: Budgeting aligns your spending with your financial goals, whether that's saving for expansion, paying off debt, or increasing your marketing efforts.

Risk Mitigation: By forecasting potential financial shortfalls, a budget enables you to prepare for and mitigate risks before they become crises.

Decision Making: With a clear budget, you can make better decisions about where to cut costs, when to invest, and how to allocate your resources most effectively.

Building Your Budget: A Step-by-Step Guide

Creating a budget that works for your business and personal finances involves several key steps:

1. Estimate Your Income: Start by forecasting your income for the budgeting period. For a business, this includes all sources of revenue, such as sales, service fees, and any other streams of income. Be realistic and, if in doubt, err on the side of caution by using conservative estimates.

2. List Your Fixed Expenses: Fixed expenses are those that remain consistent each month, such as rent or mortgage payments, utilities, insurance premiums, and salaries. These are your non-negotiable costs, so it's crucial to account for them accurately.

3. Identify Variable Expenses: Variable expenses fluctuate from month to month, such as marketing costs, travel, or inventory purchases. Review your past spending to estimate these costs and consider setting limits to prevent overspending.

4. Set Aside Savings and Investments: Allocate a portion of your income towards savings and investments. This might include building an emergency fund, saving for future expansion, or contributing to a retirement account. Treat these as non-negotiable expenses, just like your fixed costs.

5. Allocate Funds for Discretionary Spending: Discretionary spending includes non-essential items, such as entertainment, dining out, or luxury purchases. While it's important to enjoy the fruits of your labor, keeping discretionary spending in check is key to staying on budget.

6. Plan for Taxes: Don't forget to set aside money for taxes. Estimate your tax obligations based on your expected income and consider making quarterly payments to avoid a large tax bill at the end of the year.

7. Review and Adjust: Your budget is a living document. Regularly review it to ensure you're staying on track and adjust as needed. If your income fluctuates or unexpected expenses arise, update your budget to reflect these changes.

Tools and Techniques for Effective Budget Management

There are numerous tools and techniques available to help you manage your budget effectively. Here are a few that can make budgeting easier and more efficient:

Spreadsheets: Programs like Microsoft Excel or Google Sheets allow you to create custom budgets that can be easily updated and tracked. Spreadsheets are a flexible option for those who prefer to have complete control over their budget's format and structure.

Budgeting Apps: Apps like Mint, YNAB (You Need a Budget), or QuickBooks offer automated tracking of income and expenses, categorize spending, and provide visual reports to help you see where your money is going.

Envelope System: This old-school method involves allocating cash for different spending categories into physical envelopes. Once an envelope is empty, you can't spend any more in that category until the next budgeting period. This technique is especially useful for controlling discretionary spending.

Zero-Based Budgeting: With zero-based budgeting, every dollar of income is assigned a specific purpose, leaving no money unaccounted for. This method ensures that you're intentionally directing your income towards your priorities, rather than letting it slip through the cracks.

Overcoming Common Budgeting Challenges

Budgeting is not without its challenges, but understanding common pitfalls can help you avoid them:

Inconsistent Income: Many entrepreneurs face the challenge of inconsistent income, which can make budgeting difficult. To combat this, consider creating a budget based on your lowest expected monthly income, and save any surplus for months when revenue is lower.

Underestimating Expenses: It's easy to overlook or underestimate certain expenses, leading to budget shortfalls. Regularly review your past spending to ensure your budget is comprehensive, and always include a buffer for unexpected costs.

Lack of Discipline: Sticking to a budget requires discipline and commitment. To stay motivated, regularly remind yourself of your financial goals and the benefits of achieving them. Celebrate small victories along the way to reinforce positive budgeting habits.

The Role of Budgeting in Financial Success

Budgeting is more than just a financial tool—it's a habit that can lead to long-term success. By consistently managing your budget, you'll gain greater control over your finances, reduce financial stress, and position your business for sustainable growth. Whether you're just starting out or looking to refine your financial strategy, mastering budgeting is a crucial step on your path to financial independence.

Remember, a budget is not about restriction—it's about making intentional decisions that align with your goals. With a solid budget in place, you can confidently navigate the ups and downs of entrepreneurship, knowing that you have a plan to guide you toward success.

Creating a Winning Budget

Creating a winning budget is a crucial step in achieving financial success, especially as an entrepreneur. A well-structured budget not only helps you track income and expenses but also empowers you to make informed decisions that align with your business and personal goals. A winning budget is more than just a list of numbers—it's a dynamic tool that guides your financial journey, helping you allocate resources efficiently and stay focused on what truly matters.

Understanding Your Income Sources

The foundation of any budget begins with understanding your income sources. For entrepreneurs, income can come from various streams, such as sales revenue, client payments, royalties, or passive income from investments. Start by identifying all sources of income and estimating how much money you expect to earn during the budgeting period.

Be realistic when estimating your income. If your earnings fluctuate, it's wise to base your budget on a conservative estimate, such as your lowest expected income. This approach ensures that your budget remains manageable even during slower months and allows you to handle any financial surprises with confidence.

Categorizing Expenses

Once you have a clear picture of your income, the next step is to categorize your expenses. Expenses can generally be divided into two main categories: fixed and variable.

Fixed Expenses: These are expenses that remain consistent each month, such as rent, mortgage payments, utilities, insurance premiums, and salaries. Because these costs are non-negotiable, they should be prioritized in your budget.

Variable Expenses: These expenses fluctuate from month to month and include items like marketing costs, inventory purchases, travel, and entertainment. Variable expenses often provide opportunities for cost-cutting and should be closely monitored to ensure they don't exceed your budget.

Savings and Investments: A winning budget also includes provisions for savings and investments. Set aside a portion of your income for building an emergency fund, saving for future business expansion, or contributing to retirement accounts. Treat savings and investments as essential components of your budget, just like any other fixed expense.

Setting Priorities and Allocating Funds

To create a winning budget, you need to align your spending with your financial priorities. This means making intentional choices about where your money goes based on your short-term and long-term goals.

Essential Costs First: Start by allocating funds to cover your essential fixed expenses. These are the costs that keep your business and personal life running smoothly, so they should be covered first.

Prioritize Investments in Growth: Next, consider the expenses that directly contribute to the growth of your business. This might include investing in marketing, hiring new staff, or purchasing new equipment. Allocate funds to these areas strategically, ensuring that every dollar spent supports your business objectives.

Discretionary Spending: Finally, allocate funds for discretionary spending—those non-essential expenses that enhance your quality of life, like dining out, leisure activities, or luxury purchases. While it's important to enjoy the fruits of your labor, keeping discretionary spending in check is key to staying on budget and ensuring you have enough resources to invest in your business and future.

Reviewing and Adjusting Your Budget

A winning budget is not set in stone—it's a flexible tool that should evolve as your financial situation changes. Regularly review your budget to assess whether you're staying on track or if adjustments are needed. This might involve reallocating funds to different categories, cutting back on certain expenses, or adjusting your income expectations.

Monthly Reviews: Conduct a monthly review of your budget to compare your actual income and expenses with your projections. Identify any discrepancies and adjust your budget accordingly.

Adjust for Life Changes: Be prepared to adjust your budget in response to significant life or business changes, such as a new client, a change in expenses, or a personal milestone like purchasing a home. By staying flexible and proactive, you can ensure that your budget continues to serve your financial goals effectively.

Staying Committed to Your Budget

Creating a winning budget is only half the battle—sticking to it is where the real challenge lies. Commitment to your budget requires discipline and a clear understanding of your financial goals. Regularly remind yourself of why you created the budget in the first place and the long-term benefits it will bring to your financial health and business success.

Accountability: Consider sharing your budget with a trusted advisor, business partner, or financial planner who can help hold you accountable and provide guidance when needed.

Celebrate Milestones: As you reach financial milestones, take the time to celebrate your successes. This positive reinforcement can keep you motivated and committed to your budgeting process.

By following these steps, you can create a winning budget that not only helps you manage your finances effectively but also supports your business growth and personal financial well-being. Remember, a well-crafted budget is more than just a financial plan—it's a roadmap to achieving your dreams and ensuring your long-term success.

Tools and Techniques for Effective Budget Management

Budgeting is an essential skill for any entrepreneur, but it doesn't have to be a daunting task. With the right tools and techniques, managing your budget can become a streamlined and efficient process that helps you stay on track toward your financial goals. In this section, we'll explore various tools and techniques that can simplify your budgeting efforts and enhance your financial management.

Budgeting Software and Apps

In the digital age, there's no shortage of software and apps designed to help you manage your budget with ease. These tools offer features that can automate and simplify the budgeting process, making it easier to track your income, expenses, and savings in real-time. Here are some popular options:

- **QuickBooks:** A comprehensive accounting software that's particularly useful for small businesses. QuickBooks allows you to track income and expenses, generate financial reports, and even manage payroll. It's an excellent tool for entrepreneurs who want to integrate their budgeting with other financial management tasks.

- **YNAB (You Need a Budget):** YNAB is a powerful budgeting tool that encourages users to give every dollar a job, helping you to allocate funds more effectively. It's particularly popular among users who want to break the paycheck-to-paycheck cycle and gain more control over their finances.

- **Mint:** Mint is a free app that aggregates all your financial accounts in one place, giving you a complete overview of your financial situation. It automatically categorizes your expenses, tracks your spending, and provides personalized budgeting tips.

- **Google Sheets/Excel:** For those who prefer a more hands-on approach, creating a custom budget spreadsheet in Google Sheets or Excel offers maximum flexibility. You can design your budget to fit your specific needs and preferences and use built-in functions to track and analyze your financial data.

The Envelope System

The envelope system is a tried-and-true budgeting technique that involves allocating a set amount of cash to specific spending categories. While it may seem old-fashioned, this method can be incredibly effective for controlling discretionary spending and ensuring you don't exceed your budget.

- **How It Works:** Start by determining your spending categories, such as groceries, entertainment, or dining out. For each category, withdraw the budgeted amount of cash and place it in an envelope labeled with the category name. Once the cash in an envelope is gone, you cannot spend any more in that category until the next budgeting period.

- **Advantages:** The envelope system forces you to be mindful of your spending and prevents you from overspending on non-essential items. It also helps you develop better spending habits by limiting your use of credit cards and relying more on physical cash.

Zero-Based Budgeting

Zero-based budgeting is a technique where every dollar of income is assigned a specific purpose, resulting in a "zero balance" at the end of the budgeting period. This method ensures that all your income is accounted for, and that no money is left unallocated.

- **How It Works:** Start by listing your total monthly income. Next, list all your expenses, including fixed, variable, savings, and investments. Assign a dollar amount to each expense category until your total expenses equal your total income. The goal is to ensure that every dollar has a job, whether it's paying bills, saving, or investing.

- **Advantages:** Zero-based budgeting is highly effective for maintaining control over your finances and ensuring that your spending aligns with your financial goals. It encourages intentionality and prevents money from "leaking" into unplanned or unnecessary expenses.

Automation for Consistency

Consistency is key to successful budgeting, and automation can help you stay on track. Automating certain aspects of your budget ensures that critical tasks, such as saving or paying bills, are completed without fail.

Automated Savings: Set up automatic transfers from your checking account to your savings account to ensure that you're consistently setting money aside. This "pay yourself first" approach makes saving a priority and removes the temptation to spend money before you've had a chance to save it.

Automated Bill Payments: Most banks and service providers offer the option to set up automatic bill payments. This not only ensures that your bills are paid on time, avoiding late fees, but also simplifies your budgeting process by reducing the number of tasks you need to manage manually.

Regular Budget Reviews

Even with the best tools and techniques, budgeting is not a "set it and forget it" process. Regularly reviewing your budget is crucial for staying on track and making necessary adjustments as your financial situation changes.

- **Monthly Reviews:** At the end of each month, review your budget to compare your actual income and expenses against your projections. Identify any discrepancies, analyze why they occurred, and adjust your budget for the following month if needed.

- **Quarterly and Annual Reviews:** In addition to monthly reviews, conduct more in-depth reviews on a quarterly or annual basis. These reviews allow you to assess your overall financial progress, evaluate your long-term goals, and make strategic adjustments to your budget and financial plan.

Combining Techniques for Maximum Effectiveness

While each of these tools and techniques can be powerful on its own, combining them can create a robust budgeting system tailored to your specific needs. For example, you might use QuickBooks for business expenses, the envelope system for personal discretionary spending, and automate savings to ensure you're consistently building wealth.

By leveraging the right tools and techniques, you can create a budget that not only helps you manage your finances effectively but also empowers you to achieve your financial goals with confidence and clarity. Remember, the goal of budgeting is not just to track your money—it's to take control of your financial future.

CHAPTER 4

PART II: ADVANCED FINANCIAL MANAGEMENT

Saving and Investment Basics

Saving and investing are two of the most crucial components of building long-term financial security and wealth, especially for entrepreneurs. While both saving and investing involve setting aside money for the future, they serve different purposes and require different strategies. Understanding the basics of each can empower you to make informed decisions that align with your financial goals and help ensure the sustainability and growth of your business.

The Importance of Saving

Saving is the foundation of financial stability. It involves setting aside a portion of your income for future needs, emergencies, and specific goals. For entrepreneurs, having a solid savings plan is essential to navigate the uncertainties of running a business, such as fluctuating income, unexpected expenses, or economic downturns.

One of the primary purposes of saving is to build an emergency fund. An emergency fund is a reserve of money that can cover three to six months' worth of living and business expenses in case of unexpected events, such as a sudden drop in revenue, unforeseen repairs, or personal emergencies. This fund acts as a financial safety net, providing peace of mind and reducing the need to rely on credit or loans during tough times.

In addition to an emergency fund, saving is also important for achieving short-term goals, such as purchasing new equipment, investing in marketing, or expanding your business. By consistently setting aside money for these purposes, you ensure that you have the resources to seize opportunities when they arise without jeopardizing your financial health.

The Basics of Investing

While saving is about preserving your money, investing is about growing it. Investing involves putting your money into assets with the expectation that they will generate a return over time. For entrepreneurs, investing can be a powerful way to build wealth, diversify income streams, and achieve long-term financial goals.

There are several types of investments, each with its own risk and return profile. Common investment options include stocks, bonds, mutual funds, real estate, and business ventures. The key to successful investing is understanding the relationship between risk and reward. Generally, investments with higher potential returns come with higher risks, while lower-risk investments typically offer more modest returns.

Before you begin investing, it's important to assess your risk tolerance, which is your ability and willingness to endure market fluctuations and potential losses. Your risk tolerance will be influenced by factors such as your financial goals, time horizon, and overall financial situation. For example, if you're saving for retirement and have several decades before you need the funds, you might be more comfortable taking on higher-risk investments. On the other hand, if your goal is to preserve capital for a short-term need, you may prefer lower-risk options.

One of the fundamental principles of investing is diversification. Diversification involves spreading your investments across different asset classes and industries to reduce risk. By diversifying your portfolio, you minimize the impact of a poor-performing investment on your overall financial health. For example, if one of your investments underperforms, the others may perform well, balancing out your portfolio's overall performance.

Another key concept in investing is the power of compound interest. Compound interest is the process by which the returns on your investments generate earnings, and those earnings are reinvested to generate even more returns. Over time, compound interest can significantly increase the value of your investments, making it a powerful tool for building wealth.

Balancing Saving and Investing

A successful financial strategy involves both saving and investing, but the right balance between the two will depend on your individual circumstances and goals. For example, in the early stages of your business, you might prioritize building an emergency fund and saving for immediate needs. As your business grows and your financial situation stabilizes, you can shift your focus toward investing to grow your wealth and achieve long-term objectives.

It's also important to regularly review and adjust your saving and investment strategies as your circumstances change. Life events such as marriage, starting a family, or nearing retirement may prompt you to reassess your financial goals and reallocate your resources accordingly.

Starting Small and Staying Consistent

One of the biggest misconceptions about saving and investing is that you need a large sum of money to get started. The most important factor is consistency. By starting small and making regular contributions, you can build significant savings and investment portfolios over time.

For example, you might begin by setting aside a small percentage of your monthly income for savings and gradually increasing the amount as your business grows. Similarly, you can start investing with a modest sum and reinvest your earnings to take advantage of compound interest. The key is to stay disciplined and committed to your financial plan, even when progress seems slow.

The Long-Term Benefits of Saving and Investing

The benefits of saving and investing extend beyond financial security. They provide you with the freedom and flexibility to make choices that align with your values and aspirations. Whether it's expanding your business, pursuing personal passions, or achieving financial independence, saving and investing empower you to create the life you envision.

By mastering the basics of saving and investing, you lay the groundwork for a prosperous and fulfilling future. Remember, the journey to financial success is a marathon, not a sprint. With patience, persistence, and a solid strategy, you can achieve your financial goals and build lasting wealth for yourself and your business.

Why Saving Is Essential

Saving money is a fundamental aspect of financial management that every entrepreneur must prioritize. It's not just about setting aside funds for the future; it's about creating a solid financial foundation that enables you to navigate the uncertainties of business and life with confidence and resilience. The importance of saving cannot be overstated, especially for women entrepreneurs who often face unique challenges in the business world.

One of the primary reasons saving is essential is that it provides you with a financial safety net. No matter how well you plan, unexpected expenses and emergencies are inevitable. Whether it's a sudden downturn in business, an unforeseen personal expense, or an economic crisis, having a robust savings cushion can make the difference between weathering the storm or facing financial disaster. An emergency fund, typically covering three to six months of living and business expenses, offers peace of mind and ensures that you're prepared for whatever comes your way.

Beyond emergencies, saving also gives you the flexibility to seize opportunities as they arise. In business, opportunities often present themselves unexpectedly—a chance to invest in new technology, expand into a promising market, or collaborate with a strategic partner. Having savings on hand means you can act quickly and decisively, without having to scramble for financing or delay your plans. This agility can be a significant competitive advantage in the fast-paced world of entrepreneurship.

Saving is also crucial for achieving your long-term goals. Whether you're planning for retirement, saving for a major business expansion, or building wealth for your family's future, setting aside money regularly is the first step toward turning those dreams into reality. Savings allow you to make large investments without relying solely on credit or external financing, reducing your debt burden and enhancing your financial stability.

Moreover, the discipline of saving fosters a mindset of financial responsibility. It encourages you to live within your means, prioritize your spending, and think critically about your financial choices. Over time, this disciplined approach to money management becomes a habit that strengthens your overall financial health and positions you for sustained success.

For women entrepreneurs, saving is particularly important because it empowers you to maintain control over your financial future. Historically, women have faced systemic barriers to financial independence, such as limited access to capital and fewer opportunities for high-income employment. By committing to a consistent savings plan, you can build the financial resources needed to overcome these challenges, invest in your business, and secure your personal financial freedom.

In essence, saving is the bedrock of financial security. It's the practice that underpins all other financial strategies, from investing to debt management. By prioritizing saving, you're not just putting money aside—you're investing in your peace of mind, your ability to capitalize on opportunities, and your long-term financial success. As you continue your journey as an entrepreneur, remember that every dollar saved is a step closer to achieving your goals and creating the life you envision.

Introduction to Investments

Investing is one of the most powerful tools available for building wealth and achieving long-term financial goals. For women entrepreneurs, understanding the basics of investment is crucial, not just for personal financial growth, but also for the sustainability and expansion of your business. While the world of investing may seem complex and intimidating at first, it is an essential skill that can significantly enhance your financial future.

At its core, investing involves putting your money to work with the expectation of generating a return over time. Unlike saving, which is primarily about preserving capital, investing is focused on growing your wealth. This growth is achieved by purchasing assets—such as stocks, bonds, real estate, or even business ventures—that have the potential to increase in value or generate income.

One of the key concepts in investing is the relationship between risk and reward. Generally, investments that offer higher potential returns come with greater risk. For example, stocks have historically provided higher returns than savings accounts or bonds, but they also carry the risk of market volatility, where the value of your investment can fluctuate significantly. On the other hand, bonds or fixed-income investments typically offer lower returns but with less risk. Understanding your risk tolerance—the level of risk you are comfortable taking on—is essential when building your investment strategy.

Diversification is another fundamental principle in investing. Diversification involves spreading your investments across different asset classes, industries, and geographic regions to reduce risk. The idea is that by diversifying your portfolio, you protect yourself against the possibility that one poorly performing investment could significantly impact your overall financial health. For example, if you invest in a mix of stocks, bonds, and real estate, the risk is spread out, and the overall performance of your portfolio is less likely to be severely affected by a downturn in any single market.

Time is a critical factor in investing. The longer your investment horizon, the more time you must ride out market fluctuations and take advantage of compound growth. Compound growth occurs when the returns on your investments generate earnings, and those earnings are reinvested to generate even more returns. Over time, compounding can significantly boost the value of your investments, making it a powerful tool for building wealth.

For entrepreneurs, investing also means reinvesting in your own business. This might include purchasing new equipment, expanding your product line, or entering new markets. The returns on these investments can be substantial, both in terms of financial profit and business growth. However, it's important to balance business investments with other forms of investment to ensure that your wealth is not solely dependent on the success of your business.

Starting with investments doesn't require a large sum of money. Many investment platforms allow you to begin with modest amounts, and you can gradually increase your investments as your confidence and financial capacity grow. The key is to start early and stay consistent, allowing your investments to grow over time.

Understanding the basics of investing is the first step toward taking control of your financial future. By learning how to invest wisely, you can build a portfolio that not only supports your personal financial goals but also contributes to the long-term success of your business. As you explore the world of investments, remember that patience, discipline, and a willingness to learn are your greatest allies in building wealth and achieving financial independence.

CHAPTER 5

Understanding and Obtaining Credit

Credit is a critical tool in the financial toolkit of any entrepreneur, providing the flexibility and purchasing power needed to grow and sustain a business. However, understanding how credit works and knowing how to obtain it effectively are essential skills that can make the difference between using credit to your advantage and falling into financial difficulties.

At its most basic level, credit is the ability to borrow money or access goods or services with the understanding that you will repay the lender later, often with interest. For entrepreneurs, credit can come in many forms, including business loans, lines of credit, credit cards, and trade credit from suppliers. Each of these forms of credit serves different purposes, and understanding which is best suited to your needs is the first step in making smart financial decisions.

A crucial concept to grasp when it comes to credit is the difference between secured and unsecured credit. Secured credit is backed by collateral—assets like property, inventory, or equipment—that the lender can claim if you fail to repay the debt. Because secured credit is less risky for the lender, it often comes with lower interest rates and more favorable terms. Unsecured credit, on the other hand, is not backed by collateral, making it riskier for the lender and potentially more expensive for the borrower. Credit cards and personal loans are common examples of unsecured credit.

Your creditworthiness, which is your ability to repay borrowed money, plays a significant role in whether you can obtain credit and what terms you'll be offered. Lenders assess your creditworthiness by reviewing your credit score, which is a numerical representation of your credit history, and other financial factors like income, debt levels, and cash flow. A strong credit score not only increases your chances of being approved for credit but also enables you to secure better interest rates and terms, ultimately saving you money.

To build and maintain a good credit score, it's essential to manage your credit responsibly. This means making payments on time, keeping your credit card balances low relative to your credit limit, and avoiding excessive applications for new credit, which can lower your score. Regularly monitoring your credit report is also important, as it allows you to identify and correct any errors that could negatively impact your score.

When it comes to obtaining credit, preparation is key. Before applying for a loan or line of credit, ensure that your business financials are in order. This includes having up-to-date financial statements, a solid business plan, and clear documentation of your revenue streams and expenses. Lenders want to see that you have a strong grasp of your business's financial health and that you can manage credit responsibly.

Additionally, it's important to consider the purpose of the credit and how it aligns with your business goals. Are you seeking credit to fund growth, manage cash flow during a slow season, or purchase essential equipment? Understanding the purpose of the credit will help you determine the best type of credit to pursue and how much to borrow. It's crucial to borrow only what you need and what you can realistically repay, as taking on excessive debt can strain your business's finances and hinder your long-term success.

Exploring different sources of credit is also advisable. Traditional banks are a common choice for obtaining business loans, but they are not the only option. Credit unions, online lenders, and even peer-to-peer lending platforms can offer alternative financing solutions, sometimes with more flexible terms. Additionally, many small businesses leverage trade credit from suppliers, which allows you to purchase goods and pay for them later, often interest-free if paid within a certain period.

In summary, understanding and obtaining credit is about more than just accessing funds; it's about making informed decisions that support your business's financial health. By building and maintaining good credit, preparing thoroughly before applying for credit, and choosing the right type of credit for your needs, you can leverage this powerful financial tool to fuel your business's growth and success.

Types of Credit Available

Understanding the various types of credit available to you as an entrepreneur is crucial for making informed financial decisions that align with your business goals. Each type of credit serves different purposes and comes with its own set of terms, advantages, and potential risks. By familiarizing yourself with these options, you can choose the form of credit that best meets your needs and supports the growth and stability of your business.

Business Loans

Business loans are a common and often essential source of funding for entrepreneurs. These loans provide a lump sum of money that you can use for various business needs, such as purchasing equipment, expanding operations, or managing cash flow. Business loans can be secured or unsecured, with secured loans requiring collateral, such as property or inventory, and typically offering lower interest rates. Unsecured loans, while not requiring collateral, may come with higher interest rates due to the increased risk for the lender. Business loans are usually repaid over a fixed period with regular installments, making them a predictable and manageable option for many business owners.

Lines of Credit

A line of credit is a flexible form of credit that allows you to borrow up to a certain limit as needed, rather than receiving a lump sum all at once. This type of credit is particularly useful for managing cash flow fluctuations or covering short-term expenses, such as seasonal inventory purchases or unexpected repairs. You only pay interest on the amount you use, and once you repay the borrowed amount, the credit becomes available again. Lines of credit can be either secured or unsecured, with secured lines of credit typically offering better terms. The flexibility of a line of credit makes it an attractive option for businesses that need ongoing access to funds.

Credit Cards

Business credit cards are a convenient and widely used form of credit for entrepreneurs. They can be used for everyday business expenses, travel, and small purchases, providing an easy way to track and manage business spending. Many business credit cards offer rewards, such as cash back, travel points, or discounts on business-related services, which can add value to your spending. However, credit cards often come with higher interest rates than other types of credit, so it's important to use them responsibly and pay off the balance in full each month to avoid accumulating costly interest charges.

Trade Credit

Trade credit is a type of credit extended by suppliers, allowing you to purchase goods or services now and pay for them later, often within 30 to 90 days. This form of credit is commonly used in industries where maintaining inventory is crucial, such as retail or manufacturing. Trade credit can help improve your business's cash flow by giving you time to generate revenue from the goods before payment is due. Additionally, if managed well, trade credit can help build a positive credit history with suppliers, potentially leading to better terms or discounts in the future. However, failing to pay on time can damage your business relationships and credit rating, so it's important to manage trade credit carefully.

Merchant Cash Advances

A merchant cash advance (MCA) is a type of financing where a lender provides you with a lump sum of cash in exchange for a percentage of your future credit card sales. This option can be attractive to businesses with strong daily credit card sales but may be unable to qualify for traditional loans. MCAs are typically repaid through daily or weekly deductions from your credit card receipts. While merchant cash advances offer quick access to capital, they often come with high fees and interest rates, making them a more expensive form of credit. They should be used with caution and primarily as a last resort.

Peer-to-Peer Lending

Peer-to-peer (P2P) lending platforms connect borrowers directly with individual lenders, often bypassing traditional financial institutions. This type of credit can be easier to obtain for businesses that may not qualify for bank loans due to credit history or other factors. P2P loans can vary in terms of interest rates and repayment schedules, depending on the platform and the lender's assessment of your creditworthiness. While P2P lending offers flexibility and potentially lower interest rates, it's important to thoroughly research and choose reputable platforms to avoid high fees or predatory practices.

SBA Loans

Small Business Administration (SBA) loans are government-backed loans designed to help small businesses access affordable financing. SBA loans typically offer favorable terms, including lower interest rates and longer repayment periods, making them an excellent option for entrepreneurs looking to fund significant business investments. However, the application process for SBA loans can be more rigorous and time-consuming than other types of credit, as it often requires detailed financial documentation and a strong business plan.

In conclusion, the type of credit you choose will depend on your specific business needs, financial situation, and long-term goals. Whether you need short-term cash flow support or long-term financing for growth, understanding the options available to you will enable you to make the best decisions for your business's financial health and success.

Building and Maintaining a Healthy Credit Score

A healthy credit score is one of the most valuable assets an entrepreneur can possess. It's a key indicator of your creditworthiness, influencing everything from the interest rates you're offered on loans to the likelihood of securing financing for your business. Building and maintaining a strong credit score is essential for ensuring that you have access to the credit you need to grow your business, manage cash flow, and achieve your financial goals.

Understanding Your Credit Score

Your credit score is a numerical representation of your credit history, calculated using information from your credit report, such as your payment history, the amount of debt you owe, the length of your credit history, the types of credit you have, and any recent credit inquiries. The most used credit scoring model is the FICO score, which ranges from 300 to 850, with higher scores indicating better credit health.

A strong credit score generally falls within the range of 700 to 850, while scores below 650 may indicate credit risk and could lead to higher interest rates or difficulty obtaining credit. Understanding the factors that influence your credit score is the first step in managing it effectively.

Building a Strong Credit Score

Building a healthy credit score starts with establishing a positive credit history. If you're new to credit or have a limited credit history, consider opening a credit card or taking out a small loan to start building your credit. It's important to use credit responsibly by making timely payments and keeping your credit card balances low. Over time, consistent, responsible credit usage will contribute to a strong credit score.

If you already have credit, focus on making all your payments on time. Your payment history is the most significant factor in your credit score, so it's crucial to avoid late or missed payments. Setting up automatic payments or reminders can help ensure that you never miss a due date.

Another important aspect of building a strong credit score is managing your credit utilization, which is the amount of credit you're using relative to your credit limit. A general rule of thumb is to keep your credit utilization below 30%. For example, if your credit card has a $10,000 limit, aim to keep your balance under $3,000. High credit utilization can signal to lenders that you're overextended, which can negatively impact your score.

Maintaining a Healthy Credit Score

Once you've built a solid credit score, maintaining it requires ongoing attention and responsible credit management. Regularly monitor your credit report to ensure that all the information is accurate and up to date. You're entitled to a free credit report from each of the three major credit bureaus—Equifax, Experian, and TransUnion—once a year through AnnualCreditReport.com. Reviewing your credit report allows you to spot any errors or signs of identity theft early, so you can take corrective action before they damage your credit score.

Avoid opening too many new credit accounts in a short period, as multiple credit inquiries can temporarily lower your score. Additionally, applying for several new lines of credit at once can make you appear financially unstable to lenders. Instead, apply for credit only when necessary and when you're confident that it will benefit your financial situation.

It's also important to maintain a healthy mix of credit types, such as credit cards, installment loans, and mortgages. A diverse credit portfolio shows lenders that you can responsibly manage different types of credit, which can positively impact your score. However, avoid taking on credit that you don't need just to diversify your portfolio—each new account carries the potential for added debt and financial stress.

The Long-Term Benefits of a Healthy Credit Score

A strong credit score opens the door to numerous financial opportunities. With a healthy credit score, you're more likely to qualify for loans and lines of credit with favorable terms, including lower interest rates and higher credit limits. This can save you thousands of dollars in interest over the life of a loan and provide the financial flexibility you need to grow your business.

In addition to making, it easier to access credit, a good credit score can also lower your insurance premiums, improve your rental prospects, and even enhance your chances of securing business partnerships. In many ways, your credit score reflects your financial responsibility, and maintaining a strong score signals to lenders, insurers, and other financial institutions that you are a low-risk, reliable borrower.

In conclusion, building and maintaining a healthy credit score is an ongoing process that requires discipline, vigilance, and smart financial choices. By understanding how your credit score is calculated and taking proactive steps to manage it, you can ensure that your credit score remains an asset that supports your entrepreneurial journey and helps you achieve long-term financial success.

CHAPTER 6

Debt Management Strategies

Managing debt effectively is a critical skill for any entrepreneur, as it can mean the difference between maintaining financial control and facing overwhelming financial stress. While debt is often necessary for business growth—whether it's taking out loans to expand operations or using credit lines to manage cash flow—it's crucial to approach it with a clear strategy. Effective debt management not only helps you keep your business finances healthy but also positions you to leverage debt as a tool for growth rather than a burden.

Understanding Your Debt

The first step in managing debt is to thoroughly understand your current debt situation. This involves taking stock of all your outstanding debts, including business loans, credit card balances, lines of credit, and any other obligations. For each debt, know the interest rate, the remaining balance, the minimum monthly payment, and the payment due dates. By having a complete picture of your debt, you can begin to prioritize which debts to address first and develop a plan to pay them off systematically.

Prioritizing Debt Repayment

Not all debt is created equal, and prioritizing which debts to pay off first can save you money in the long run. A common approach is to focus on high-interest debt first, such as credit cards or high-interest personal loans. By paying down these debts more aggressively, you reduce the total amount of interest you'll pay overtime, which can free up cash flow for other financial goals.

Another strategy is the "debt snowball" method, which involves paying off the smallest debts first, regardless of interest rate. This approach can provide psychological benefits by giving you quick wins, which can boost your motivation and confidence to tackle larger debts. Once the smallest debt is paid off, you roll that payment into the next smallest debt, creating a snowball effect that accelerates your progress.

Refinancing and Consolidation

If you're struggling to manage multiple debts with high interest rates, refinancing or consolidating your debt may be an option. Refinancing involves taking out a new loan with better terms—such as a lower interest rate or longer repayment period—to pay off an existing loan. This can reduce your monthly payments and overall interest costs, making your debt more manageable.

Debt consolidation, on the other hand, involves combining multiple debts into a single loan with one monthly payment. This simplifies your debt repayment process and can sometimes result in a lower overall interest rate. However, it's important to be cautious with consolidation—while it can make payments more manageable, it doesn't eliminate the debt, and in some cases, it could extend the repayment period, leading to more interest paid overtime.

Creating a Repayment Plan

A key element of successful debt management is having a clear and realistic repayment plan. Start by setting a budget that prioritizes debt repayment while still covering your essential business and personal expenses. Determine how much you can allocate each month toward paying down your debts and stick to this plan consistently.

Consider making extra payments whenever possible, especially on high-interest debt. Even small additional payments can reduce the principal balance faster, which lowers the total interest you'll pay. Automating your debt payments can also help ensure you never miss a due date, which could result in late fees and damage to your credit score.

Avoiding Future Debt Pitfalls

Effective debt management is not just about paying off current debt; it's also about avoiding unnecessary debt in the future. Before taking on new debt, carefully evaluate whether it's truly necessary and how it aligns with your business goals. Consider alternative financing options, such as seeking investment, improving cash flow management, or cutting costs, before resorting to borrowing.

Maintaining a strong credit score is also essential for managing debt effectively. A healthy credit score can help you secure lower interest rates and better terms on any future borrowing, making debt more manageable. Regularly review your credit report, keep your credit utilization low, and pay off your balances in full whenever possible.

The Psychological Aspect of Debt Management

Debt can be a significant source of stress, especially for entrepreneurs who are responsible not only for their financial well-being but also for the livelihoods of their employees. Managing debt requires a balance of financial acumen and emotional resilience. It's important to address any feelings of anxiety or overwhelm that debt may cause and to seek support if needed—whether from a financial advisor, a mentor, or a support network of fellow entrepreneurs.

Remember that managing debt is a process, and it's okay to adjust your strategies as your financial situation evolves. By staying disciplined, proactive, and focused on your long-term financial goals, you can successfully navigate your debt and build a stronger, more resilient business.

How to Manage and Reduce Debt

Effectively managing and reducing debt is crucial for maintaining financial health and ensuring the long-term success of your business. Debt, when managed wisely, can be a valuable tool for growth; however, if left unchecked, it can quickly become a burden that limits your financial flexibility and peace of mind. The key to debt management lies in adopting a proactive approach that not only addresses existing obligations but also prevents future debt from spiraling out of control.

Assess Your Current Debt Situation

The first step in managing and reducing debt is to take a comprehensive look at your current financial obligations. Gather all the details about your debts, including outstanding balances, interest rates, minimum payments, and due dates. Create a list or spreadsheet that clearly outlines this information, giving you a full view of your debt landscape. This process will help you understand where you stand financially and identify which debts need the most immediate attention.

Prioritize Your Debts

Once you have a clear picture of your debts, the next step is to prioritize them based on factors like interest rates and outstanding balances. Two common strategies for prioritizing debt repayment are:

High-Interest Debt First: Focus on paying off debts with the highest interest rates first, as these are the costliest over time. By reducing high-interest debt, you can decrease the total amount of interest you pay and free up more money to address other financial goals.

Debt Snowball Method: Alternatively, you might choose to pay off the smallest debts first, regardless of interest rate. This method allows you to achieve quick wins, building momentum and motivation to tackle larger debts.

Decide which strategy aligns best with your financial situation and personal preferences and commit to it.

Create a Repayment Plan

A well-structured repayment plan is essential for reducing debt systematically. Start by determining how much you can realistically allocate each month toward debt repayment without compromising your other financial obligations. Consider setting aside any additional income—such as bonuses, tax refunds, or side gig earnings—exclusively for debt repayment to accelerate the process.

Ensure that your repayment plan includes making at least the minimum payments on all debts to avoid late fees and negative impacts on your credit score. If possible, make extra payments on your prioritized debts to reduce the principal balance faster, which can significantly shorten the repayment period.

Negotiate with Creditors

If you're struggling to manage your debt, consider reaching out to your creditors to negotiate more favorable terms. Many lenders are willing to work with borrowers who demonstrate a genuine effort to repay their debts. You might negotiate lower interest rates, reduced monthly payments, or even a settlement amount that is less than the total owed. While not always guaranteed, successful negotiations can make your debt more manageable and provide some relief.

Consider Consolidation or Refinancing

Debt consolidation and refinancing are strategies that can simplify your repayment process and potentially lower your interest rates.

Debt Consolidation: This involves combining multiple debts into a single loan with one monthly payment, which can help you manage your debt more efficiently. Look for consolidation loans that offer lower interest rates than your existing debts to reduce the overall cost.

Refinancing: Refinancing involves taking out a new loan with better terms—such as a lower interest rate or extended repayment period—to pay off existing debts. This can decrease your monthly payments and free up cash flow, although it may extend the repayment period, resulting in more interest paid overtime.

Cut Expenses and Increase Income

Reducing your debt often requires finding extra money to put toward repayment. Start by examining your current expenses and identifying areas where you can cut back. This might involve scaling back non-essential business expenses, renegotiating contracts with suppliers, or delaying discretionary spending until your debt is under control.

In addition to cutting costs, consider ways to increase your income. This could include taking on additional projects, offering new products or services, or finding passive income streams. The extra income generated can then be dedicated entirely to reducing your debt, accelerating your progress.

Stay Committed and Monitor Progress

Debt reduction is a marathon, not a sprint, and staying committed to your repayment plan is crucial. Regularly review your progress and adjust your strategy if necessary. Celebrate small victories along the way, such as paying off a credit card or reaching a milestone in your repayment plan, to keep yourself motivated.

It's also important to monitor your credit report throughout the process to ensure that your efforts are reflected in an improved credit score. Regular monitoring can help you catch and correct any errors that could negatively impact your credit.

Avoid Taking on New Debt

Finally, one of the most important aspects of debt management is avoiding the accumulation of new debt while you're focused on repayment. Before taking on additional debt, consider whether it's necessary and how it will affect your overall financial health. Aim to live within your means and only borrow when it strategically benefits your business or aligns with your long-term financial goals.

By following these strategies, you can effectively manage and reduce your debt, creating a more secure financial foundation for your business. Remember, the journey to becoming debt-free requires patience, discipline, and a clear plan, but the rewards—financial freedom, reduced stress, and greater flexibility—are well worth the effort.

Negotiating with Creditors

When managing debt becomes overwhelming, negotiating with creditors can be an effective strategy to ease your financial burden. Creditors, from credit card companies to lenders, often prefer to negotiate rather than risk non-payment, especially when you demonstrate a proactive approach to resolving your debt. Successful negotiations can lead to lower interest rates, reduced monthly payments, or even a settlement for less than the total amount owed, providing much-needed relief and helping you regain control of your finances.

Assess Your Situation

Before reaching out to creditors, it's crucial to have a clear understanding of your financial situation. Review your debts, including the balances, interest rates, and monthly payments. Identify which debts are causing the most strain on your finances and prioritize those for negotiation. Also, take stock of your income, expenses, and any financial changes that have impacted your ability to make payments. This preparation will allow you to approach negotiations with a clear, realistic proposal.

Contact Your Creditors Early

The sooner you communicate with your creditors, the better. If you foresee difficulty in making upcoming payments, it's wise to reach out before you fall behind. Creditors are generally more willing to negotiate when you're current on your payments or only slightly behind, as it shows you're taking responsibility for your financial obligations. Be honest about your situation and explain why you're struggling to meet the current terms. Express your willingness to pay and your desire to find a solution that works for both parties.

Know What You Want

Before entering negotiations, have a clear idea of what you want to achieve. Are you looking for a lower interest rate, an extended repayment period, or a temporary reduction in payments? Perhaps you're seeking a settlement where you pay a lump sum that's less than the total owed. Knowing your goals will help you stay focused during negotiations and make it easier to reach a mutually beneficial agreement.

Be Prepared to Negotiate

Negotiating with creditors is a two-way conversation, and it's important to be flexible and open to compromise. Start by proposing a realistic solution based on what you can afford. For example, if your goal is to reduce your monthly payments, explain how much you can reasonably pay and suggest a payment plan that reflects that amount. If you're negotiating a lower interest rate, mention competitive rates offered by other lenders or your desire to remain a loyal customer.

Creditors may counter with offers that don't fully meet your needs, so be prepared to discuss alternatives and negotiate terms that work for both sides. Stay calm, patient, and professional throughout the conversation. Remember, the goal is to reach an agreement that helps you manage your debt more effectively while maintaining a positive relationship with the creditor.

Get Everything in Writing

Once you've reached an agreement with a creditor, it's crucial to get all the details in writing. This documentation should outline the new terms, including the adjusted payment amounts, interest rates, and any other agreed-upon conditions. Having everything in writing protects you in case of future disputes and ensures that both parties are clear on the terms of the agreement.

Review the written agreement carefully before signing, and don't hesitate to ask for clarification if anything is unclear. Keep a copy of the agreement for your records and make sure to follow through with the new payment plan as agreed.

Consider Professional Help

If negotiating with creditors feels overwhelming or if you're dealing with multiple creditors, you might benefit from professional assistance. Credit counseling agencies, debt settlement companies, and financial advisors can help you navigate negotiations, create a debt management plan, and advocate on your behalf. However, be sure to choose reputable professionals with a track record of helping clients successfully manage debt.

Follow Through and Stay Committed

After negotiating new terms with your creditors, it's essential to stay committed to the agreement. Make your payments on time and in full to avoid falling back into financial trouble. If your situation changes and you're unable to keep up with the new terms, contact your creditor immediately to discuss further adjustments. Demonstrating responsibility and consistent effort will help you rebuild trust with your creditors and improve your overall financial health.

Negotiating with creditors can be a powerful tool for managing debt, but it requires preparation, persistence, and clear communication. By approaching negotiations strategically and staying committed to your agreements, you can alleviate financial stress and take significant steps toward reducing your debt and achieving long-term financial stability.

CHAPTER 7

Navigating Funding Opportunities

Securing the right funding is a critical component of growing and sustaining a successful business. Whether you're launching a new venture, expanding your operations, or managing cash flow, understanding the various funding opportunities available to you is essential. As a woman entrepreneur, navigating the world of business funding can be particularly challenging, but with the right knowledge and approach, you can access the resources you need to take your business to the next level.

Understanding Your Funding Needs

The first step in navigating funding opportunities is to clearly define your business's financial needs. Are you seeking capital to start a new business, expand an existing one, or cover operational costs? Understanding the purpose of the funding will help you determine the amount needed and identify the most suitable sources of financing. Additionally, consider your repayment capacity and the timeline for when the funds will be needed. Being clear about your needs will allow you to target the right funding options and present a compelling case to potential lenders or investors.

Traditional Financing Options

Traditional financing options, such as bank loans and lines of credit, remain popular choices for many entrepreneurs. Banks offer a range of loan products, including term loans, which provide a lump sum of capital to be repaid over a fixed period, and lines of credit, which allow you to borrow as needed up to a certain limit. These options are ideal for businesses with a solid financial history and collateral to secure the loan.

However, securing traditional financing can be challenging, particularly for new businesses or those with less established credit histories. It often requires a detailed business plan, financial statements, and personal guarantees. Despite these challenges, traditional financing offers relatively low-interest rates and longer repayment terms, making it an attractive option if you can meet the criteria.

Alternative Financing Options

If traditional financing isn't a viable option, there are several alternative funding sources to consider. These options often provide more flexibility and faster access to capital, though they may come with higher costs.

Online Lenders: Online lenders have become a popular alternative to traditional banks, offering a range of loan products with more lenient eligibility requirements. They often provide quicker approval and funding, making them an excellent option for businesses that need fast access to capital. However, interest rates can be higher, so it's important to compare offers and understand the terms.

Crowdfunding: Crowdfunding platforms, such as Kickstarter or Indiegogo, allow you to raise funds from many people, often in exchange for rewards or early access to products. This option is particularly appealing for creative projects or products with strong consumer appeal. Successful crowdfunding campaigns can also serve as marketing tools, generating buzz and building a customer base before your product even launches.

Angel Investors and Venture Capitalists: For businesses with high growth potential, angel investors and venture capitalists (VCs) can provide significant funding in exchange for equity in your company. Angel investors are typically high-net-worth individuals who invest their own money, while VCs manage pooled funds from multiple investors. While these options offer substantial capital, they often come with expectations of rapid growth and a high return on investment. Additionally, you may need to give up some control of your business in exchange for the funding.

Grants and Competitions: Many organizations offer grants and business competitions specifically targeted at women entrepreneurs. Unlike loans, grants do not need to be repaid, making them highly desirable. However, they are often competitive and require a strong application, including a clear business plan and evidence of your business's impact. Research available grants in your industry or region and take the time to craft a compelling application.

Preparing for the Funding Process

No matter which funding option you pursue, preparation is key to success. Start by ensuring your business plan is robust and up to date, with clear financial projections, a detailed market analysis, and a strong value proposition. Lenders and investors want to see that you have a thorough understanding of your business, your market, and how you plan to achieve your goals.

Next, gather all necessary documentation, including financial statements, tax returns, and personal credit reports. Being organized and ready with the required information will make the application process smoother and demonstrate your professionalism to potential funders.

Finally, be prepared to pitch your business. Whether you're applying for a loan, seeking investment, or entering a competition, you'll need to articulate why your business is worth funding. Practice your pitch, focusing on the key points that highlight your business's strengths and potential for success.

Navigating the Challenges

Securing funding is often one of the most challenging aspects of entrepreneurship, particularly for women who may face additional barriers in accessing capital. It's important to remain persistent and resourceful, exploring all available options and not being discouraged by setbacks. Networking can also play a crucial role in finding funding opportunities—connecting with other entrepreneurs, attending industry events, and joining business organizations can open doors to potential funders and valuable advice.

In conclusion, navigating funding opportunities requires a clear understanding of your business's needs, thorough preparation, and a willingness to explore various financing options. By approaching the process strategically, you can secure the funding necessary to fuel your business's growth and achieve your entrepreneurial goals.

Finding the Right Funding for Your Business

Securing the right funding is a pivotal decision that can significantly impact the trajectory of your business. The right type of funding aligns with your business goals, supports your growth strategy, and ensures financial stability. However, with so many options available—from traditional loans to alternative financing—it's essential to carefully assess your needs and choose the funding that best suits your specific situation.

Assess Your Business Needs

The first step in finding the right funding is to clearly define why you need the capital. Are you launching a new product, expanding into a new market, or simply looking to stabilize cash flow? Understanding the purpose of the funding will guide you toward the most appropriate financing options. For example, if you need short-term funding to cover operational expenses during a slow season, a line of credit might be more suitable than a long-term loan. Conversely, if you're planning a major expansion, a term loan or investment might provide the substantial capital required.

Consider the Stage of Your Business

Your business's stage of development also plays a crucial role in determining the right funding. Startups often have different funding needs than established businesses. Early-stage businesses may benefit from seed funding, angel investors, or crowdfunding, where the focus is on raising initial capital to bring a product or service to market. Established businesses with a proven track record might pursue more traditional financing options, such as bank loans or lines of credit, to fund expansion or scale operations.

Evaluate the Cost of Capital

It's important to understand the cost associated with each funding option. This includes not only the interest rate but also any fees, the repayment schedule, and the total cost over time. For example, while online lenders may offer quick access to capital, they often come with higher interest rates compared to traditional bank loans. Similarly, equity financing from venture capitalists may not involve immediate repayment but requires giving up a portion of your business ownership, which can be costly in terms of long-term control and profits.

Calculate the total cost of each funding option and consider how it fits within your financial projections. The goal is to find funding that is not only affordable but also sustainable for your business in the long run.

Align with Your Business Goals

The right funding should align with both your short-term and long-term business goals. For instance, if your goal is to rapidly scale your business, venture capital might provide the significant investment needed to fuel growth, along with strategic guidance and industry connections. On the other hand, if your goal is to maintain full control of your business while managing cash flow, a business line of credit or traditional loan might be more appropriate.

Consider how each funding option will affect your business operations, decision-making, and future opportunities. Aligning your choice of funding with your broader business objectives ensures that the capital you raise will effectively support your vision for growth and success.

Consider Flexibility and Control

Another key factor to consider is the level of flexibility and control each funding option offers. Debt financing, such as loans and lines of credit, typically allows you to retain full ownership of your business, but it comes with the obligation of regular repayments, which can impact cash flow. Equity financing, on the other hand, provides capital without immediate repayment but requires sharing ownership and decision-making with investors.

Think about how much control you want to maintain over your business and how flexible you need your financing to be. If maintaining control is a top priority, you might lean towards debt financing. If you're comfortable with bringing on partners who can contribute more than just capital—such as expertise and connections—equity financing might be a better fit.

Research and Compare Options

Finally, take the time to research and compare different funding options. Look beyond the obvious choices and explore lesser-known alternatives, such as grants, microloans, or industry-specific funding programs. Each option has its own advantages and challenges, and what works for one business may not work for another. Speak with financial advisors, attend funding workshops, and network with other entrepreneurs to gain insights and advice.

By thoroughly evaluating your business needs, goals, and the available funding options, you can make a well-informed decision that supports your business's growth and financial health. The right funding isn't just about accessing capital—it's about finding a partner in your business's journey to success.

Grant and Loan Opportunities

Accessing the right financial resources is critical for women entrepreneurs looking to start or expand their businesses. Among the many options available, grants and loans stand out as two of the most common and effective means of securing funding. Each option offers unique benefits and challenges, and understanding how to navigate these opportunities can significantly enhance your ability to finance your business ventures.

Grants: Free Capital with a Competitive Edge

Grants are highly sought-after funding sources because they provide capital that does not need to be repaid. For women entrepreneurs, grants can be particularly attractive as they often target underrepresented groups in business, including women-owned businesses. However, grants are typically competitive and require a well-crafted application that demonstrates a clear business plan, potential for impact, and alignment with the grantor's goals.

There are various types of grants available, including:

- **Government Grants:** Federal, state, and local governments offer grants to support small businesses, especially those owned by women, minorities, and other underrepresented groups. Programs like the Small Business Innovation Research (SBIR) and Small Business Technology Transfer (STTR) grants are examples of government initiatives designed to foster innovation and economic growth.

- **Private and Corporate Grants:** Many private foundations and corporations offer grants to women entrepreneurs. These organizations often seek to support businesses that align with their corporate social responsibility goals or that operate in specific industries, such as technology, healthcare, or sustainable development.

- **Industry-Specific Grants:** Certain industries have specialized grants available to businesses that meet specific criteria, such as agriculture, tech startups, or creative arts. Researching industry-specific opportunities can uncover unique funding sources tailored to your business niche.

Applying for grants requires time and effort, but the rewards can be substantial. Successful grant applications typically include a detailed business plan, financial projections, and a clear explanation of how the grant funds will be used to achieve specific business objectives. It's also important to meet all eligibility requirements and adhere to application deadlines. Persistence and attention to detail can increase your chances of securing grant funding.

Loans: Flexible Financing with Clear Repayment Terms

Loans are another essential funding option for women entrepreneurs. Unlike grants, loans must be repaid with interest, but they offer greater flexibility and accessibility. Loans can provide the capital needed to start a new business, expand operations, or cover operational costs during challenging periods.

There are several types of loans available, each with its own terms and conditions:

- **Traditional Bank Loans:** Banks and credit unions offer a range of loan products tailored to small businesses, including term loans, lines of credit, and equipment financing. These loans often have competitive interest rates and clear repayment schedules, making them a reliable option for businesses with solid credit and financial history.

- **Small Business Administration (SBA) Loans:** The SBA provides government-backed loans that are designed to support small businesses. SBA loans typically offer favorable terms, such as lower interest rates and longer repayment periods, making them accessible to businesses that may not qualify for traditional bank loans. The SBA 7(a) loan program and SBA Microloan program are popular options for women entrepreneurs seeking financing.

- **Microloans:** Microloans are small, short-term loans typically offered by nonprofit organizations or community lenders. These loans are designed to help businesses that need a modest amount of capital, often for specific purposes like purchasing equipment or covering initial startup costs. Microloans are particularly beneficial for entrepreneurs who may have limited credit history or are just starting out.

- **Online and Alternative Lenders:** The rise of online lending platforms has made it easier for entrepreneurs to access loans quickly and with less stringent requirements. These platforms often offer a range of loan products, from short-term working capital loans to long-term business loans. However, interest rates may be higher than traditional loans, so it's important to carefully review the terms before committing.

Choosing Between Grants and Loans

When deciding between grants and loans, consider the specific needs and circumstances of your business. Grants offer the advantage of free capital, but they are competitive and often require detailed applications. Loans, while requiring repayment, provide more immediate access to funds and can be tailored to meet the specific financial needs of your business.

In some cases, combining both grants and loans may be the best approach. For example, you might use a grant to fund a specific project or initiative while securing a loan to cover broader operational costs. This strategy allows you to leverage the strengths of each funding type while minimizing their respective drawbacks.

In conclusion, navigating the world of grants and loans requires a clear understanding of your business needs, diligent research, and careful planning. By exploring and applying for the right opportunities, you can secure the financial resources necessary to grow your business and achieve your entrepreneurial goals.

CHAPTER 8

Part III: Financial Risks and Protection

Investment Strategies for Growth

Investing is a critical component of long-term business growth and financial success. For women entrepreneurs, developing effective investment strategies can help you expand your business, build wealth, and secure your financial future. Whether you're reinvesting profits back into your business, diversifying into new ventures, or building a personal investment portfolio, the right strategies can accelerate your growth and maximize your returns.

Reinvesting in Your Business

One of the most straightforward and impactful investment strategies is to reinvest profits back into your business. Reinvestment can take many forms, such as upgrading equipment, expanding your product line, hiring additional staff, or increasing your marketing efforts. Each of these investments can contribute directly to your business's growth by enhancing efficiency, boosting sales, or expanding your market reach.

When reinvesting in your business, it's important to prioritize opportunities that offer the highest potential return on investment (ROI). For example, investing in technology that automates processes or improves customer experience can lead to significant cost savings and increased revenue. Similarly, entering new markets or launching innovative products can open up new revenue streams and help you stay competitive in a rapidly changing business landscape.

Diversifying Your Investment Portfolio

While reinvesting in your business is crucial, it's equally important to diversify your investments to manage risk and build long-term wealth. Diversification involves spreading your investments across different asset classes, industries, and geographic regions to reduce the impact of any single investment's poor performance on your overall financial health.

A well-diversified portfolio might include a mix of stocks, bonds, real estate, and other investment vehicles. For entrepreneurs, diversification can also involve investing in other businesses or industries outside your core area of expertise. This strategy not only reduces risk but also provides opportunities to benefit from growth in different sectors.

For example, if your business operates in the technology sector, you might consider investing in real estate or healthcare to balance your exposure. By diversifying, you protect your wealth from the volatility of any one market and increase the likelihood of achieving consistent returns over time.

Leveraging Compound Interest

One of the most powerful investment strategies for long-term growth is leveraging the power of compound interest. Compound interest occurs when the returns on your investments generate earnings, and those earnings are reinvested to generate even more returns. Over time, this compounding effect can significantly increase the value of your investments, making it a key driver of wealth accumulation.

To maximize the benefits of compound interest, start investing as early as possible and contribute regularly to your investment accounts. Even small, consistent contributions can grow substantially over time, thanks to the compounding effect. For example, setting up automatic contributions to a retirement account or investment fund ensures that you're consistently building wealth, even during periods of market volatility.

Balancing Risk and Reward

Every investment carries a degree of risk, and understanding your risk tolerance is essential for developing a growth-oriented investment strategy. Higher-risk investments, such as stocks or venture capital, offer the potential for higher returns but also come with greater volatility. Lower-risk investments, like bonds or savings accounts, provide more stability but typically offer lower returns.

As an entrepreneur, you may be more comfortable with risk, given the nature of running a business. However, it's important to balance your investment portfolio according to your financial goals, time horizon, and overall risk tolerance. A diversified portfolio that includes a mix of high-risk and low-risk investments can help you achieve growth while protecting your assets from significant losses.

Staying Informed and Adapting Your Strategy

The investment landscape is constantly evolving, and staying informed about market trends, economic conditions, and emerging opportunities is crucial for success. Regularly reviewing and adjusting your investment strategy ensures that it remains aligned with your goals and responsive to changes in the market.

Consider working with a financial advisor or investment professional who can provide guidance and help you navigate complex investment decisions. Additionally, continuing your financial education by attending workshops, reading industry publications, and participating in investment communities can enhance your knowledge and confidence as an investor.

Long-Term Perspective and Patience

Investing for growth requires a long-term perspective and the patience to weather market fluctuations. It's important to avoid making impulsive decisions based on short-term market movements, as these can undermine your overall investment strategy. Instead, focus on your long-term goals and remain committed to your investment plan, knowing that growth takes time and persistence.

In conclusion, effective investment strategies are essential for driving business growth, building wealth, and achieving financial independence. By reinvesting in your business, diversifying your portfolio, leveraging compound interest, and balancing risk with reward, you can create a solid foundation for long-term success. With a disciplined approach and a commitment to continuous learning, you can navigate the complexities of investing and turn your financial goals into reality.

Stocks, Bonds, and Mutual Funds

When it comes to building a diversified investment portfolio, stocks, bonds, and mutual funds are fundamental components that offer varying levels of risk and reward. Understanding how these financial instruments work and how they can fit into your investment strategy is essential for achieving long-term financial growth.

Stocks: Ownership with Growth Potential

Stocks represent shares of ownership in a company. When you purchase a stock, you're essentially buying a small piece of that company, which entitles you to a portion of its profits. Stocks are known for their potential to generate high returns over time, making them a popular choice for growth-oriented investors.

However, with the potential for higher returns comes greater risk. The value of stocks can be highly volatile, fluctuating based on a company's performance, industry trends, and broader economic conditions. While stocks can appreciate significantly, they can also lose value, sometimes rapidly. For this reason, investing in stocks is generally recommended for those with a higher risk tolerance and a long-term investment horizon.

Diversifying your stock investments across different industries, sectors, and geographic regions can help mitigate risk. By not putting all your eggs in one basket, you reduce the impact of any single company's poor performance on your overall portfolio.

Bonds: Stability and Income

Bonds are debt securities issued by corporations, municipalities, or governments to raise capital. When you purchase a bond, you are essentially lending money to the issuer in exchange for periodic interest payments and the return of the bond's face value at maturity. Bonds are generally considered lower-risk investments compared to stocks, making them a staple for those seeking stability and regular income.

The primary benefit of bonds is their relative stability. They tend to be less volatile than stocks and provide a steady stream of income through interest payments, which can be particularly appealing during periods of economic uncertainty. However, bonds typically offer lower returns than stocks, so they might not be sufficient as a sole investment for long-term growth.

There are different types of bonds, each with varying levels of risk and return. Government bonds, such as U.S. Treasury bonds, are considered among the safest investments, as they are backed by the government. Corporate bonds, issued by companies, offer higher yields but come with higher risk, especially if the issuing company's financial health is in question.

Mutual Funds: Diversification Made Simple

Mutual funds are investment vehicles that pool money from multiple investors to purchase a diversified portfolio of stocks, bonds, or other securities. Managed by professional portfolio managers, mutual funds offer a convenient way to invest in a broad range of assets without having to buy each one individually.

One of the primary advantages of mutual funds is diversification. Because a mutual fund invests in a variety of assets, it helps spread risk across different investments. This diversification can protect your portfolio from the significant impact of a single investment's poor performance.

Mutual funds come in various types, each with different investment objectives. Equity mutual funds focus on stocks and aim for capital growth, while bond mutual funds invest in fixed-income securities to provide steady income. Balanced mutual funds, which invest in a mix of stocks and bonds, offer a compromise between growth and income, appealing to investors who seek both.

Mutual funds are also accessible, as they typically require lower minimum investments compared to buying individual stocks or bonds. However, they do come with management fees, which can vary depending on the fund. It's important to review these fees, as they can impact your overall returns.

Choosing the Right Mix for Your Portfolio

Stocks, bonds, and mutual funds each play a unique role in a diversified investment portfolio. The right mix of these assets depends on your financial goals, risk tolerance, and time horizon. For example, a younger investor with a long-term growth focus might allocate a larger portion of their portfolio to stocks, while someone nearing retirement might prioritize bonds and income-focused mutual funds to preserve capital and generate income.

Regularly reviewing and adjusting your portfolio is essential to ensure it remains aligned with your goals and market conditions. As your financial situation evolves, you may need to rebalance your portfolio to maintain the right balance of risk and reward.

In conclusion, understanding and investing in stocks, bonds, and mutual funds is key to building a robust and resilient investment strategy. By carefully selecting and managing these investments, you can achieve a balanced portfolio that supports both your business and personal financial objectives, paving the way for long-term success.

Real Estate and Other Investment Vehicles

Real estate and alternative investment vehicles offer entrepreneurs additional avenues for diversifying their portfolios and generating wealth. While these investments often require more capital and can involve greater complexity, they also provide unique benefits, such as passive income, capital appreciation, and protection against inflation. Understanding these options and how they fit into your overall investment strategy can significantly enhance your financial growth and stability.

Real Estate: Tangible Assets with Long-Term Value

Investing in real estate has long been a popular strategy for building wealth. Real estate investments involve purchasing physical properties, such as residential homes, commercial buildings, or land, with the potential to generate income through rental payments or to appreciate over time.

One of the primary advantages of real estate is its ability to generate consistent, passive income. Rental properties, for instance, can provide a steady cash flow, which can be particularly valuable for entrepreneurs looking to supplement their business income. Additionally, real estate often appreciates in value over the long term, offering the potential for significant capital gains when properties are sold.

Real estate also serves as a hedge against inflation. As the cost of living rises, property values and rental income typically increase as well, helping to preserve the purchasing power of your investment. Moreover, real estate investments can be leveraged—meaning you can borrow money to purchase a property, potentially amplifying your returns.

However, real estate investments come with challenges, including the need for substantial initial capital, ongoing maintenance costs, and the risk of property value fluctuations. Managing real estate can also be time-consuming, particularly if you're handling tenant relations and property upkeep yourself. For these reasons, many investors choose to work with property management companies or invest in real estate through Real Estate Investment Trusts (REITs), which offer exposure to real estate without the hands-on management.

Other Investment Vehicles: Exploring Alternative Opportunities

Beyond traditional stocks, bonds, and real estate, there are a variety of alternative investment vehicles that can further diversify your portfolio and provide unique opportunities for growth. These include:

Commodities: Investing in commodities like gold, silver, oil, or agricultural products can provide a hedge against inflation and currency fluctuations. Commodities tend to perform well during periods of economic uncertainty, making them a useful addition to a diversified portfolio.

Private Equity: Private equity involves investing directly in private companies, either through purchasing equity stakes or providing capital for growth. This type of investment is typically more complex and illiquid than public stocks, but it offers the potential for significant returns, particularly if the company experiences substantial growth or is acquired.

Venture Capital: Like private equity, venture capital involves investing in early-stage startups with high growth potential. While venture capital can be risky, with many startups failing to achieve profitability, successful investments can result in outsized returns. For entrepreneurs with industry expertise, venture capital can also provide opportunities to mentor and guide new businesses.

Peer-to-Peer Lending: Peer-to-peer (P2P) lending platforms allow you to lend money directly to individuals or small businesses in exchange for interest payments. This investment vehicle can offer higher returns than traditional savings accounts or bonds, but it also carries a higher risk of default.

Cryptocurrency: Cryptocurrency, such as Bitcoin or Ethereum, is a digital or virtual currency that uses cryptography for security. While still a relatively new and volatile asset class, cryptocurrency has attracted significant attention as a potential investment. However, its high volatility and regulatory uncertainties make it a high-risk investment, suitable only for those with a high tolerance for risk.

Balancing Traditional and Alternative Investments

Incorporating real estate and other alternative investment vehicles into your portfolio can enhance diversification and open up new avenues for growth. However, these investments often come with higher risks and require a deeper understanding of the markets involved. It's important to balance these investments with more traditional assets, such as stocks and bonds, to manage risk effectively.

Before diving into real estate or alternative investments, take the time to educate yourself, seek advice from financial professionals, and assess how these investments align with your financial goals and risk tolerance. By carefully selecting and managing a mix of traditional and alternative investments, you can build a robust, diversified portfolio that supports your long-term financial success.

In conclusion, real estate and other investment vehicles offer valuable opportunities for growth and diversification. When approached strategically, these investments can provide a powerful complement to your broader financial strategy, helping you achieve a well-rounded and resilient investment portfolio.

CHAPTER 9

Risk Management

Risk management is a crucial aspect of financial planning and business strategy, especially for entrepreneurs navigating the complexities of growing and sustaining a business. Every business faces risks—whether financial, operational, legal, or market-related—and how you manage these risks can significantly impact your business's long-term success and stability. Effective risk management involves identifying potential risks, assessing their impact, and implementing strategies to mitigate them, ensuring that your business is resilient in the face of uncertainty.

Identifying Potential Risks

The first step in risk management is identifying the various risks your business might face. These can be categorized into several broad types:

Financial Risks: These include risks related to cash flow, credit, interest rates, and investments. For example, a sudden drop in revenue or an unexpected increase in costs could jeopardize your business's financial health.

Operational Risks: These involve risks related to your business's day-to-day operations, such as supply chain disruptions, equipment failure, or employee turnover. Operational risks can lead to delays, increased costs, or a decline in product or service quality.

Market Risks: Market risks stem from changes in the broader market environment, such as shifts in consumer demand, new competitors entering the market, or economic downturns. These risks can affect your sales, pricing strategies, and overall market position.

Legal and Regulatory Risks: Compliance with laws and regulations is essential for avoiding legal penalties and reputational damage. Legal risks include potential lawsuits, intellectual property disputes, or changes in regulations that could impact your business operations.

Reputational Risks: A business's reputation is one of its most valuable assets. Reputational risks can arise from negative publicity, customer complaints, or ethical breaches, all of which can lead to a loss of trust and, ultimately, customers.

Assessing the Impact

Once you've identified potential risks, the next step is to assess their impact on your business. This involves evaluating both the likelihood of each risk occurring and the potential severity of its consequences. Not all risks are equal—some may be unlikely but catastrophic if they occur, while others may be more common but have less severe consequences.

A common approach to risk assessment is to create a risk matrix, which plots the likelihood of a risk on one axis and its impact on the other. This visual tool can help you prioritize which risks addressing first, focusing your efforts on those that pose the greatest threat to your business.

Mitigating Risks

After assessing the risks, it's time to develop strategies to mitigate them. Risk mitigation involves taking proactive steps to reduce the likelihood of a risk occurring or to minimize its impact if it does. Here are some common risk mitigation strategies:

Diversification: In financial risk management, diversification—whether in investments, suppliers, or revenue streams—helps spread risk and reduce the impact of any single event on your business.

Insurance: Insurance is a key tool for managing financial risks. Depending on your business, you may need property insurance, liability insurance, or specialized policies like cyber insurance. Insurance can provide financial protection against significant losses, helping your business recover from unexpected events.

Contingency Planning: Developing contingency plans for high-impact risks ensures that your business can respond quickly and effectively if a risk materializes. This might include having backup suppliers, maintaining an emergency fund, or creating crisis communication protocols.

Strong Internal Controls: Implementing strong internal controls, such as regular audits, clear policies, and employee training, can help prevent operational and legal risks. Internal controls ensure that your business operates efficiently and in compliance with regulations.

Regular Monitoring and Review: Risk management is an ongoing process. Regularly monitoring your business environment and reviewing your risk management strategies helps you stay prepared for new and evolving risks. This continuous review process allows you to adapt your strategies as needed, ensuring that your business remains resilient.

Embracing Risk as Part of Growth

While risk management is about minimizing potential downsides, it's also important to recognize that taking risks is an inherent part of entrepreneurship. Not all risks should be avoided—some risks are necessary for growth and innovation. The key is to take calculated risks, where the potential rewards justify the exposure to risk.

Effective risk management doesn't mean eliminating all risks; rather, it means understanding the risks you face, preparing for them, and making informed decisions that balance risk with opportunity. By adopting a proactive approach to risk management, you can protect your business from unexpected challenges while positioning it to seize new opportunities for growth.

In conclusion, risk management is a vital discipline for any entrepreneur. By identifying, assessing, and mitigating risks, you can ensure that your business is prepared to navigate uncertainties and continue to thrive in a competitive marketplace. This strategic approach not only safeguards your business's financial health but also empowers you to make bold, confident decisions that drive long-term success.

Identifying Financial Risks

Identifying financial risks is a critical first step in safeguarding your business and ensuring its long-term success. Financial risks are those uncertainties that can negatively impact your business's financial health, ranging from cash flow issues to market fluctuations. By recognizing and understanding these risks, you can develop strategies to manage them effectively and protect your business from potential financial instability.

Cash Flow Risks

One of the most common financial risks faced by entrepreneurs is cash flow risk. Cash flow refers to the movement of money in and out of your business, and maintaining a healthy cash flow is essential for covering daily operations, paying employees, and investing in growth. Cash flow risks arise when there is a mismatch between incoming revenue and outgoing expenses, leading to periods of insufficient cash to meet obligations. This can occur due to delayed payments from clients, unexpected expenses, or seasonal fluctuations in sales.

To identify cash flow risks, regularly monitor your cash flow statements and look for patterns or trends that could signal potential issues. Understanding your business's cash flow cycle—how long it takes for cash to flow in from sales and out for expenses—can help you anticipate and mitigate periods of shortfall.

Credit Risks

Credit risk refers to the potential for losses due to the failure of customers, clients, or partners to fulfill their financial obligations. This risk is particularly relevant if your business extends credit to customers, allowing them to pay for goods or services at a later date. If customers delay payments or default on their obligations, it can strain your cash flow and impact your ability to pay your own bills.

To manage credit risks, assess the creditworthiness of potential customers before extending credit, set clear payment terms, and establish a system for monitoring and collecting overdue accounts. Diversifying your customer base can also reduce your exposure to credit risk, as your financial stability will not be overly dependent on a single client or group of clients.

Interest Rate Risks

Interest rate risk arises from fluctuations in interest rates that can affect your business's cost of borrowing and investment returns. If your business relies on loans or credit lines with variable interest rates, an increase in interest rates could lead to higher borrowing costs, which may reduce profitability. Conversely, if you invest in interest-bearing assets, falling interest rates could diminish your investment income.

Identifying interest rate risks involves reviewing your debt obligations and investment portfolios to understand how sensitive they are to changes in interest rates. Consider the potential impact of rising or falling rates on your business and explore options such as locking in fixed interest rates or diversifying your investments to mitigate this risk.

Market Risks

Market risk refers to the possibility of financial losses due to changes in market conditions, such as shifts in consumer demand, economic downturns, or increased competition. Market risks can affect your business's revenue, pricing strategies, and overall market position. For instance, an economic recession could lead to reduced consumer spending, while new competitors entering the market could erode your market share.

To identify market risks, stay informed about industry trends, economic indicators, and competitor activities. Conduct regular market research to understand how changes in the market environment could impact your business. Having a flexible business model that can adapt to changing market conditions is key to mitigating market risks.

Currency Risks

If your business operates internationally or deals with foreign currencies, currency risk—or exchange rate risk—can be a significant concern. Currency risk arises when fluctuations in exchange rates affect the value of transactions conducted in foreign currencies. For example, if the value of the currency you receive declines relative to your home currency, you may receive less revenue than expected, impacting your profitability.

To identify currency risks, assess the extent to which your business is exposed to foreign currencies and consider the impact of exchange rate fluctuations on your financial statements. Strategies to manage currency risk include using hedging instruments, such as forward contracts or options, to lock in exchange rates, or diversifying your currency exposure to spread the risk.

Liquidity Risks

Liquidity risk occurs when your business is unable to meet short-term financial obligations due to a lack of liquid assets—cash or assets that can quickly be converted to cash. Even profitable businesses can face liquidity risks if their assets are tied up in long-term investments or if they have insufficient working capital to cover immediate expenses.

Identifying liquidity risks involves regularly reviewing your balance sheet to ensure that you have sufficient liquid assets to cover short-term liabilities. Maintaining an emergency fund or securing a line of credit can provide a financial cushion to manage liquidity risks.

In conclusion, identifying financial risks is an essential practice for every entrepreneur. By understanding the various financial risks your business may face—cash flow, credit, interest rate, market, currency, and liquidity risks—you can take proactive steps to mitigate these risks and ensure the financial stability and resilience of your business. Effective risk management begins with awareness, followed by strategic planning to address potential challenges before they become critical issues.

Mitigation Strategies

Mitigation strategies are essential tools for managing and minimizing the impact of the various risks your business may face. As a woman entrepreneur, implementing effective mitigation strategies can help you navigate uncertainties, protect your financial health, and ensure the continuity of your business operations. These strategies involve proactive planning, diversification, and the use of financial instruments to reduce exposure to risk.

Diversification

One of the most effective ways to mitigate financial risk is through diversification. Diversifying your revenue streams, customer base, and investments helps spread risk and reduces the likelihood that a single event will significantly impact your business. For example, if your business relies heavily on one key client, consider expanding your client base to avoid being overly dependent on that single source of revenue. Similarly, in your investment portfolio, spreading investments across different asset classes, industries, and geographic regions can protect against market volatility.

Insurance

Insurance is a critical component of any risk management strategy. By transferring specific risks to an insurance provider, you can protect your business from significant financial losses due to unforeseen events. Key types of insurance to consider include:

General Liability Insurance: Protects against claims of bodily injury, property damage, and personal injury related to your business operations.

Professional Liability Insurance: Covers legal expenses and damages if your business is sued for negligence or errors in the services provided.

Property Insurance: Protects your business property, including buildings and equipment, against risks such as fire, theft, and natural disasters.

Business Interruption Insurance: Covers lost income and operating expenses if your business is temporarily unable to operate due to a covered event.

Assess your business's specific risks and ensure you have adequate coverage to mitigate potential losses.

Contingency Planning

Contingency planning involves preparing for potential risks by developing backup plans that can be activated in the event of a disruption. A well-thought-out contingency plan allows your business to respond quickly and effectively to crises, minimizing downtime and financial losses. For instance, if your primary supplier experiences a disruption, having alternative suppliers lined up can prevent supply chain issues from affecting your operations. Similarly, maintaining an emergency fund or access to credit can provide the liquidity needed to manage unexpected expenses or cash flow shortfalls.

Hedging

Hedging is a financial strategy used to reduce exposure to risks, such as fluctuations in currency exchange rates, interest rates, or commodity prices. By using financial instruments like futures contracts, options, or swaps, you can lock in prices or rates, thereby reducing the uncertainty of future costs or revenues. For businesses that operate internationally or rely on volatile commodities, hedging can be an effective way to stabilize cash flow and protect profit margins.

Strong Internal Controls

Implementing strong internal controls is vital for mitigating operational and financial risks. Internal controls are procedures and policies designed to ensure the integrity of financial reporting, prevent fraud, and promote efficient operations. Examples include:

Segregation of Duties: Ensures that no single employee has control over all aspects of a financial transaction, reducing the risk of errors or fraud.

Regular Audits: Conducting regular internal and external audits helps identify potential issues early and ensures compliance with accounting standards and regulations.

Clear Policies and Procedures: Establishing and enforcing clear policies for financial transactions, record-keeping, and reporting reduces the risk of errors and inconsistencies.

By maintaining robust internal controls, you can safeguard your business's assets and ensure accurate financial reporting.

Regular Risk Assessment and Review

Risk management is not a one-time activity but an ongoing process. Regularly assessing and reviewing the risks your business faces allow you to adapt your mitigation strategies as needed. As your business grows and the market environment changes, new risks may emerge, and existing risks may evolve. By staying vigilant and proactive, you can continuously improve your risk management practices and ensure your business remains resilient.

In conclusion, effective risk mitigation requires a combination of strategic planning, diversification, financial tools, and ongoing vigilance. By implementing these mitigation strategies, you can protect your business from potential threats, reduce the impact of unforeseen events, and position your business for long-term success.

CHAPTER 10

Insurance Essentials

Insurance is a cornerstone of risk management, providing a vital safety net that protects your business from unexpected events and financial losses. As a woman entrepreneur, understanding and securing the right types of insurance is essential to safeguarding your business, assets, and personal liability. The right coverage not only provides peace of mind but also ensures that your business can recover quickly in the event of a disruption.

General Liability Insurance

General liability insurance is fundamental for any business, offering protection against claims of bodily injury, property damage, and personal injury that could arise from your business operations. This type of insurance covers legal fees, medical expenses, and settlements or judgments if your business is found liable. Whether you operate from a physical location or provide services at clients' sites, general liability insurance shields your business from significant financial risks associated with accidents or damages.

Professional Liability Insurance

Also known as errors and omissions (E&O) insurance, professional liability insurance is crucial for businesses that provide expert services or advice. This coverage protects you from claims of negligence, mistakes, or failure to deliver promised services. For example, if a client alleges that your advice led to financial loss, professional liability insurance would cover legal defense costs and any damages awarded. This type of insurance is especially important for consultants, freelancers, and professionals in fields like law, accounting, and healthcare.

Property Insurance

Property insurance covers the physical assets of your business, including buildings, equipment, inventory, and furniture, against risks such as fire, theft, vandalism, and natural disasters. If your business premises are damaged or your inventory is destroyed, property insurance can help cover the costs of repairs or replacements, minimizing the financial impact on your operations. Even if you operate a home-based business, it's essential to have property insurance, as homeowners' policies often do not cover business-related assets.

Business Interruption Insurance

Business interruption insurance, also known as business income insurance, is designed to protect your business from income loss due to a covered event that forces you to temporarily close or scale back operations. This type of insurance covers lost income, ongoing expenses such as rent and payroll, and sometimes even the costs associated with relocating your business temporarily. For example, if a fire damages your office, business interruption insurance would help you cover the financial gap while you rebuild and get back to full operations.

Workers' Compensation Insurance

If your business has employees, workers' compensation insurance is typically required by law. This insurance provides medical benefits and wage replacement to employees who are injured or become ill as a result of their job. Workers' compensation also protects your business from lawsuits related to workplace injuries, offering financial protection in the event of a workplace accident. Ensuring that you have adequate workers' compensation coverage is not only a legal requirement but also a key element of protecting your business and employees.

Cyber Liability Insurance

In today's digital age, cyber liability insurance is increasingly important, especially for businesses that handle sensitive customer data or rely heavily on digital operations. This insurance covers the costs associated with data breaches, cyberattacks, and other cyber incidents, including legal fees, notification costs, and expenses related to restoring compromised data. As cyber threats continue to evolve, having cyber liability insurance can protect your business from the potentially devastating financial consequences of a cyber incident.

Key Person Insurance

Key person insurance is a type of life insurance that provides financial protection to your business in the event of the death or disability of a key employee, such as a founder, executive, or top salesperson. The insurance payout can be used to cover the costs of recruiting and training a replacement, as well as to compensate for lost income or business disruptions. For small businesses where one or two individuals are crucial to operations, key person insurance can be a critical safeguard.

Choosing the Right Coverage

Selecting the right insurance coverage involves assessing your business's unique risks and needs. It's important to work with a knowledgeable insurance agent or broker who can help you identify potential exposures and tailor an insurance package that provides comprehensive protection. Regularly reviewing and updating your insurance coverage as your business grows and evolves ensures that you remain adequately protected against emerging risks.

In conclusion, securing the right insurance is essential for protecting your business against unforeseen events that could otherwise result in significant financial losses. By understanding the various types of insurance available and choosing the coverage that aligns with your business needs, you can mitigate risks and focus on growing your business with confidence.

Types of Insurance You Need

As a woman entrepreneur, protecting your business from potential risks is paramount to ensuring its longevity and success. Having the right insurance coverage is a critical component of your risk management strategy. The types of insurance you need will depend on the nature of your business, the industry you operate in, and the specific risks you face. Here are the essential types of insurance that every entrepreneur should consider:

General Liability Insurance

General liability insurance is the foundation of any business insurance plan. It covers claims related to bodily injury, property damage, and personal injury that may occur on your business premises or as a result of your operations. Whether you operate from a physical location or provide services offsite, this insurance is crucial for protecting your business from lawsuits and financial loss.

Professional Liability Insurance

If your business provides professional services or advice, professional liability insurance—also known as errors and omissions (E&O) insurance—is essential. This coverage protects against claims of negligence, mistakes, or failure to deliver services as promised. It's particularly important for consultants, lawyers, accountants, and other professionals whose clients rely on their expertise.

Property Insurance

Property insurance covers the physical assets of your business, including buildings, equipment, inventory, and furniture. It protects against risks such as fire, theft, vandalism, and natural disasters. Even if you operate a home-based business, property insurance is important, as standard homeowners' policies may not cover business-related assets.

Business Interruption Insurance

Business interruption insurance helps cover lost income and ongoing expenses if your business is forced to close temporarily due to a covered event, such as a fire or natural disaster. This insurance ensures that you can continue to meet financial obligations, such as rent and payroll, while your business recovers.

Workers' Compensation Insurance

If you have employees, workers' compensation insurance is typically required by law. It provides medical benefits and wage replacement to employees who are injured or become ill as a result of their job. Workers' compensation also protects your business from lawsuits related to workplace injuries, making it a key element of your overall risk management strategy.

Cyber Liability Insurance

In today's digital landscape, cyber liability insurance is increasingly important, especially if your business handles sensitive customer data or relies heavily on digital operations. This insurance covers the costs associated with data breaches, cyberattacks, and other cyber incidents, including legal fees and the cost of restoring compromised data.

Key Person Insurance

Key person insurance provides financial protection in the event of the death or disability of a key employee, such as a founder or top executive. The insurance payout can be used to cover the costs of recruiting and training a replacement and to compensate for lost income or business disruptions. This type of insurance is crucial for small businesses where a few key individuals are vital to the company's success.

Commercial Auto Insurance

If your business owns or uses vehicles, commercial auto insurance is necessary to protect against accidents, theft, and liability related to business vehicle use. This insurance covers damages to your vehicles, as well as liability for injuries or property damage caused by your vehicles.

Product Liability Insurance

If your business manufactures or sells products, product liability insurance protects against claims of injury or damage caused by your products. This coverage is essential for businesses involved in product design, manufacturing, distribution, or retail.

Directors and Officers (D&O) Insurance

For businesses with a board of directors or executive team, D&O insurance provides protection against claims related to the decisions and actions of company leaders. It covers legal fees and damages arising from lawsuits alleging breach of duty, negligence, or wrongful acts by directors or officers.

In conclusion, the types of insurance you need depend on the specific risks associated with your business. By securing the appropriate coverage, you can protect your business from potential financial losses, ensure compliance with legal requirements, and focus on growing your business with confidence. Regularly reviewing and updating your insurance coverage as your business evolves will help you stay prepared for any challenges that may arise.

Understanding Policies and Claims

Understanding your insurance policies and the process for filing claims is essential to ensuring that your business is adequately protected and can recover quickly in the event of a loss. As a woman entrepreneur, it's important to be well-informed about the terms and conditions of your insurance coverage, as well as how to navigate the claims process effectively. By mastering these aspects, you can make informed decisions, avoid common pitfalls, and maximize the benefits of your insurance protection.

Reading and Comprehending Your Insurance Policies

Insurance policies can be complex documents filled with legal and technical jargon. However, it's crucial to thoroughly read and understand the terms of your policies to know exactly what is covered, what is excluded, and the conditions under which a claim can be made. Key elements of an insurance policy include:

Declarations Page: This section provides an overview of the policy, including the insured party, coverage limits, and premium amounts. It's important to verify that all information on the declarations page is accurate.

Coverage Details: This section outlines what risks and events are covered by the policy. For example, a general liability policy might cover bodily injury and property damage but exclude certain types of incidents, such as pollution or professional errors.

Exclusions: Exclusions are specific situations or risks that are not covered by the policy. Understanding these exclusions helps you identify potential gaps in coverage that you may need to address with additional policies.

Endorsements and Riders: These are modifications to the standard policy that either extend or limit coverage. Endorsements can be added to tailor the policy to your specific needs, such as increasing coverage limits or adding coverage for specific risks.

Conditions: The conditions section outlines the responsibilities of both the insurer and the insured. It includes requirements such as timely premium payments, maintaining certain safety standards, and reporting incidents promptly.

The Claims Process

Knowing how to file a claim and what to expect during the claims process is critical for receiving the benefits of your insurance coverage when you need it most. The claims process generally involves the following steps:

Immediate Notification: As soon as an incident occurs that may lead to a claim, notify your insurance provider immediately. Prompt notification is often a condition of coverage, and delays can result in the denial of the claim.

Documentation and Evidence: Gather all relevant documentation and evidence related to the incident, such as photos, videos, receipts, and witness statements. Detailed records help substantiate your claim and speed up the process.

Filing the Claim: Submit a formal claim to your insurance provider, providing all necessary details about the incident and the resulting damages or losses. Your insurer will assign a claims adjuster to investigate the claim and determine the extent of coverage.

Working with the Adjuster: The claims adjuster will assess the damage, review your documentation, and may request additional information. It's important to cooperate fully and provide any requested information promptly to avoid delays.

Claim Resolution: Once the adjuster has completed their investigation, the insurer will decide on the claim. If approved, the insurer will issue a payment based on the terms of your policy. If the claim is denied or the payment is less than expected, you have the right to appeal the decision or negotiate a settlement.

Avoiding Common Pitfalls

To avoid common pitfalls in managing your policies and claims, consider the following best practices:

Regular Policy Reviews: Regularly review your insurance policies to ensure they still meet your business needs, especially as your business grows or changes. Adjust coverage as necessary to avoid underinsurance or gaps in protection.

Accurate and Honest Reporting: Always provide accurate and honest information when applying for insurance or filing a claim. Misrepresentation can lead to claim denial or policy cancellation.

Maintain Records: Keep organized records of all insurance-related documents, including policies, payment receipts, correspondence with insurers, and claims documentation. These records are invaluable if disputes arise.

Understand Your Deductibles: Be aware of the deductibles on your policies—the amount you are responsible for paying out of pocket before insurance coverage kicks in. Ensure that your business can comfortably cover these amounts in the event of a claim.

In conclusion, understanding your insurance policies and the claims process is essential for making the most of your insurance protection. By being proactive in reading your policies, maintaining proper documentation, and following best practices during the claims process, you can ensure that your business is well-protected and able to recover swiftly from any setbacks.

CHAPTER 11

Legal Considerations

Navigating the legal landscape is a critical aspect of running a successful business, particularly for women entrepreneurs who must ensure that their ventures are compliant with laws and regulations. Legal considerations touch every part of your business, from how you structure your company to how you protect your intellectual property and handle contracts. Understanding and addressing these legal issues proactively can help you avoid costly disputes, protect your assets, and maintain a strong foundation for growth.

Business Structure

One of the first legal decisions you'll need to make as an entrepreneur is choosing the right business structure. The structure you choose—whether it's a sole proprietorship, partnership, limited liability company (LLC), or corporation—will affect your personal liability, taxation, and the way you manage your business. For example:

- **Sole Proprietorship:** Simple and easy to set up but offers no separation between your personal and business assets, leaving you personally liable for business debts.

- **Partnership:** Involves shared ownership and liability with one or more partners. It's important to have a clear partnership agreement to define roles, responsibilities, and profit-sharing.

- **LLC:** Offers flexibility in management and provides personal liability protection, meaning your personal assets are generally protected from business debts and claims.

- **Corporation:** A more complex structure that provides the highest level of personal liability protection but comes with stricter regulatory requirements and potential double taxation (corporate income taxed separately from shareholder dividends).

Choosing the right structure is crucial for minimizing risk and optimizing tax benefits. Consulting with a legal advisor or business attorney can help you make the best choice based on your specific circumstances.

Contracts and Agreements

Contracts are the backbone of business transactions, ensuring that all parties understand their rights and obligations. Whether you're dealing with suppliers, clients, employees, or partners, having well-drafted contracts is essential for protecting your interests and preventing disputes. Key considerations include:

- **Clarity:** Contracts should clearly outline the terms of the agreement, including payment terms, delivery schedules, and performance expectations. Avoid vague language that could lead to misunderstandings.

- **Compliance:** Ensure that your contracts comply with applicable laws and regulations, particularly in areas such as employment, consumer rights, and data protection.

- **Enforceability:** A contract is only useful if it's enforceable. Make sure your contracts are legally binding and include provisions for dispute resolution, such as mediation or arbitration, to address issues if they arise.

- **Confidentiality and Non-Compete Clauses:** Protect your business's proprietary information and competitive edge by including confidentiality agreements and non-compete clauses in contracts with employees, contractors, and partners.

Intellectual Property Protection

Intellectual property (IP) is one of the most valuable assets of any business, encompassing everything from your brand name and logo to proprietary products, processes, and creative works. Protecting your IP is essential for maintaining your competitive advantage. Consider the following steps:

- Trademarks: Register your business name, logo, and any distinctive branding elements as trademarks to protect them from being used by others.

- **Patents:** If your business has developed a unique product or process, consider applying for a patent to protect your invention from being copied or exploited by competitors.

- **Copyrights:** Protect creative works such as written content, designs, and software with copyright registration, ensuring that you retain control over how your work is used and distributed.

- **Trade Secrets:** Safeguard sensitive business information, such as customer lists, formulas, or strategies, by implementing strict confidentiality agreements and internal controls.

Employment Law

As your business grows and you hire employees, it's important to comply with employment laws that govern wages, working conditions, and employee rights. Key areas to consider include:

- **Hiring Practices:** Ensure that your hiring practices are fair, non-discriminatory, and compliant with labor laws. This includes creating clear job descriptions, conducting background checks legally, and understanding the rules around interviewing and hiring.

- **Wage and Hour Laws:** Adhere to minimum wage laws, overtime requirements, and regulations regarding working hours. Misclassifying employees as independent contractors to avoid these obligations can lead to legal issues.

- **Workplace Policies:** Develop comprehensive workplace policies, including those related to harassment, discrimination, health and safety, and employee benefits. Make sure these policies are communicated to employees and enforced consistently.

- **Termination Procedures:** Follow legal procedures when terminating employees to avoid wrongful termination claims. This includes documenting performance issues, providing notice as required by law, and offering severance where appropriate.

Regulatory Compliance

Depending on your industry, your business may be subject to a range of regulations, from health and safety standards to environmental laws and data protection requirements. It's essential to stay informed about the regulations that apply to your business and ensure compliance to avoid fines, legal action, and damage to your reputation.

In conclusion, legal considerations are a fundamental part of running a successful business. By understanding the legal landscape, protecting your intellectual property, ensuring regulatory compliance, and drafting strong contracts, you can mitigate risks and position your business for long-term success. Working with legal professionals and staying proactive in managing legal issues will help you navigate the complexities of entrepreneurship with confidence.

Legal Structures for Business

Choosing the right legal structure for your business is one of the most important decisions you'll make as an entrepreneur. The legal structure you select will have significant implications for your personal liability, tax obligations, and the way your business is managed and operated. Understanding the different legal structures available can help you make an informed decision that aligns with your business goals and provides the necessary protections and advantages.

Sole Proprietorship

A sole proprietorship is the simplest and most common legal structure for small businesses. In this structure, there is no distinction between the owner and the business—the owner is personally responsible for all debts, liabilities, and obligations of the business.

- **Advantages:** Easy and inexpensive to set up, complete control over business decisions, straightforward tax reporting (income is reported on the owner's personal tax return).
- **Disadvantages:** Unlimited personal liability, meaning the owner's personal assets are at risk if the business incurs debt or legal issues; limited ability to raise capital.

Partnership

A partnership is a legal structure where two or more individuals share ownership of a business. Partnerships can be general, where all partners are equally responsible for the business, or limited, where some partners have limited liability and involvement in management.

- **Advantages:** Simple to establish, shared responsibility and resources, potential for greater capital and expertise, profits pass through to partners and are taxed on their individual tax returns.
- **Disadvantages:** Unlimited personal liability for general partners, potential for conflicts between partners, shared profits, and decision-making.

Limited Liability Company (LLC)

An LLC is a flexible legal structure that combines the liability protection of a corporation with the tax benefits and simplicity of a partnership. Owners of an LLC, known as members, are protected from personal liability for the business's debts and obligations.

- **Advantages:** Limited personal liability for members, flexible management structure, pass-through taxation (profits are taxed on members' personal tax returns), fewer compliance requirements than a corporation.
- **Disadvantages:** May have higher setup costs and more paperwork than a sole proprietorship or partnership, profits are subject to self-employment taxes unless the LLC opts for corporate taxation.

Corporation

A corporation is a more complex legal structure where the business is a separate legal entity from its owners (shareholders). This separation provides the highest level of personal liability protection but comes with more regulatory requirements.

- **Advantages:** Limited personal liability for shareholders, ability to raise capital through the sale of stock, perpetual existence (the corporation continues to exist even if ownership changes), potential tax advantages (e.g., lower corporate tax rates).
- **Disadvantages:** More expensive and complex to set up, subject to double taxation (corporate profits are taxed, and dividends paid to shareholders are also taxed), extensive record-keeping and regulatory compliance required.

S Corporation

An S Corporation is a special type of corporation that allows profits to pass through to the shareholders' personal tax returns, avoiding double taxation. To qualify as an S Corporation, the business must meet specific IRS requirements, including limits on the number and type of shareholders.

- **Advantages:** Limited personal liability, avoidance of double taxation, ability to raise capital, perpetual existence.
- **Disadvantages:** Strict eligibility requirements, limited to 100 shareholders (who must be U.S. citizens or residents), more regulatory requirements than an LLC.

Nonprofit Organization

A nonprofit organization is a legal structure for businesses that operate for charitable, educational, religious, or other public purposes. Nonprofits can apply for tax-exempt status, meaning they are not required to pay federal income taxes on profits related to their mission.

- **Advantages:** Tax-exempt status, eligibility for grants and donations, limited liability for directors and officers, potential for public recognition and support.
- **Disadvantages:** Strict regulatory requirements, profits must be reinvested in the organization's mission rather than distributed to owners or shareholders, complex setup process.

Choosing the Right Structure

Selecting the right legal structure depends on various factors, including the size and nature of your business, your financial goals, the level of personal liability you're willing to assume, and your plans for growth. Consulting with a business attorney or accountant can provide valuable guidance in making this decision, ensuring that you choose a structure that best supports your business objectives and provides the necessary legal and financial protections.

In conclusion, understanding the different legal structures available for your business is crucial for setting a strong foundation for success. By carefully considering your options and seeking professional advice, you can choose a structure that aligns with your needs, protects your interests, and positions your business for long-term growth.

Protecting Your Business Legally

Ensuring that your business is legally protected is a fundamental aspect of entrepreneurship, particularly for women navigating the complexities of the business world. Legal protection goes beyond simply choosing the right structure for your business; it involves a proactive approach to safeguarding your intellectual property, enforcing contracts, adhering to regulations, and minimizing liability risks. By taking the necessary legal precautions, you can protect your assets, secure your business's future, and focus on growth with confidence.

One of the most crucial steps in legally protecting your business is securing your intellectual property (IP). This includes trademarks, patents, copyrights, and trade secrets that are vital to your brand and operations. Registering trademarks for your business name, logo, and other branding elements prevents others from using them, ensuring that your brand identity remains distinct and protected. If your business involves innovation, such as unique products or processes, obtaining patents is essential to prevent competitors from copying your ideas. Similarly, copyrights protect your creative works, including written content, designs, and software, ensuring that you maintain control over their use and distribution.

Contracts play a key role in protecting your business relationships and transactions. Every agreement, whether it's with clients, suppliers, or employees, should be formalized in a well-drafted contract that clearly outlines the terms, expectations, and responsibilities of all parties involved. A strong contract not only provides clarity but also serves as a legal safeguard in case of disputes. It's important to work with a legal professional to ensure that your contracts are comprehensive and enforceable, covering areas such as payment terms, confidentiality, and dispute resolution.

Regulatory compliance is another critical aspect of legal protection. Depending on your industry, your business may be subject to various regulations, from health and safety standards to environmental laws and data protection requirements. Non-compliance can result in fines, legal action, and reputational damage. Staying informed about the regulations that apply to your business and implementing the necessary policies and procedures to comply with them is essential for avoiding legal troubles and maintaining your business's integrity.

Minimizing liability risks is also a key component of legal protection. This involves taking steps to limit your personal liability as well as the business's exposure to legal claims. Choosing the right legal structure, such as an LLC or corporation, is the first step in separating your personal assets from your business liabilities. Additionally, having the right insurance coverage—such as general liability, professional liability, and workers' compensation—provides a financial safety net in the event of accidents, errors, or other unforeseen incidents.

Finally, ongoing legal monitoring and review are crucial for ensuring that your business remains protected as it grows and evolves. Regularly reviewing contracts, updating IP registrations, and staying current with regulatory changes help you adapt to new risks and opportunities. By maintaining a proactive legal strategy, you can navigate the complexities of entrepreneurship with greater confidence and security.

In conclusion, protecting your business legally requires a comprehensive and proactive approach. By securing your intellectual property, enforcing contracts, ensuring regulatory compliance, and minimizing liability, you can safeguard your business's assets and position it for long-term success. Legal protection is not just about avoiding risks—it's about empowering your business to thrive in a competitive and dynamic environment.

CHAPTER 12

Part IV: Planning for the Future

Tax Planning and Benefits

Effective tax planning is a critical component of financial management for any entrepreneur. It involves more than just filing your taxes on time—it's about strategically managing your finances to minimize your tax liability and maximize the benefits available to your business. For women entrepreneurs, understanding and leveraging the tax planning opportunities specific to your business structure and industry can result in significant cost savings, freeing up resources to reinvest in growth.

The foundation of tax planning begins with choosing the right business structure, as different structures offer varying tax advantages. For instance, a sole proprietorship allows you to report business income and expenses on your personal tax return, simplifying the filing process. However, an LLC or S Corporation might offer more opportunities to reduce self-employment taxes, especially if your business generates substantial profits. Understanding how your business structure impacts your tax obligations is crucial for optimizing your tax strategy.

One of the most effective ways to reduce your tax burden is by taking advantage of all available deductions and credits. Common deductions for businesses include expenses related to operating costs, such as rent, utilities, and office supplies. If you work from home, you may also qualify for a home office deduction, which allows you to deduct a portion of your home expenses, like mortgage interest and utilities, based on the percentage of your home used for business. Additionally, keep track of expenses related to travel, meals, and entertainment that are directly related to your business, as these can also be deducted.

Beyond deductions, tax credits can significantly reduce the amount of taxes you owe. Unlike deductions, which lower your taxable income, credits reduce your tax bill dollar-for-dollar. For example, if your business invests in renewable energy or provides health insurance to employees, you might qualify for specific tax credits. It's important to stay informed about the credits available to small businesses, as these can change from year to year based on new legislation.

Retirement planning is another area where tax benefits can play a significant role. Contributing to a retirement plan, such as a Simplified Employee Pension (SEP) IRA, Solo 401(k), or SIMPLE IRA, not only helps secure your financial future but also offers immediate tax advantages. Contributions to these plans are typically tax-deductible, reducing your taxable income for the year. Additionally, the growth of investments within these retirement accounts is tax-deferred, meaning you won't pay taxes on the earnings until you withdraw the funds in retirement.

It's also essential to consider the timing of income and expenses when planning for taxes. By strategically timing income recognition and expense payments, you can manage your tax liability from year to year. For example, if you anticipate being in a higher tax bracket next year, you might accelerate expenses or defer income to reduce your tax burden in the current year. This approach requires careful forecasting and a deep understanding of your business's cash flow and profit projections.

Working with a qualified tax advisor or accountant is invaluable in navigating the complexities of tax planning. A professional can help you identify opportunities to save, ensure compliance with tax laws, and develop a tax strategy that aligns with your overall business goals. They can also assist with tax-efficient business decisions, such as the timing of major purchases or investments, and advise on the potential tax implications of business expansion or restructuring.

In conclusion, tax planning is an essential aspect of managing your business's finances. By understanding the tax implications of your business structure, taking full advantage of deductions and credits, and strategically managing income and expenses, you can reduce your tax liability and enhance your business's financial health. Effective tax planning not only helps you keep more of what you earn but also positions your business for long-term growth and success.

Preparing for Tax Season

Tax season can be a stressful time for entrepreneurs, but with proper preparation, it can also be an opportunity to maximize your tax savings and ensure compliance with tax regulations. Preparing for tax season involves more than just gathering receipts—it requires a proactive approach to organizing your financial records, understanding your tax obligations, and leveraging the available deductions and credits to minimize your tax liability. By taking the time to prepare thoroughly, you can avoid last-minute scrambling and set your business up for a smooth and successful tax filing process.

The foundation of effective tax preparation is maintaining accurate and up-to-date financial records throughout the year. This includes tracking all income, expenses, and business-related transactions in a systematic way. Whether you use accounting software, spreadsheets, or a professional bookkeeper, having organized records ensures that you can easily access the information needed to file your taxes accurately. Make it a habit to regularly reconcile your accounts, categorize expenses correctly, and keep digital copies of important documents, such as invoices, receipts, and bank statements.

Understanding your tax obligations is another critical aspect of preparing for tax season. Depending on your business structure, you may be responsible for federal, state, and local taxes, including income tax, self-employment tax, payroll tax, and sales tax. It's important to know the specific tax deadlines that apply to your business and to plan accordingly. For example, if you're a sole proprietor or single-member LLC, your business income is reported on your personal tax return, and quarterly estimated tax payments may be required to avoid penalties. If you have employees, you'll also need to ensure that payroll taxes are filed and paid on time.

Maximizing deductions and credits is key to reducing your tax liability. As tax season approaches, review your financial records to identify all eligible deductions, such as home office expenses, business travel, and equipment purchases. Consider meeting with a tax advisor to explore any additional deductions or credits you may qualify for, such as those related to health insurance, retirement contributions, or energy-efficient improvements. Your tax advisor can also help you strategize the timing of certain expenses to optimize your tax situation, such as making end-of-year purchases or deferring income.

Tax planning isn't just about the current tax year—it's also about positioning your business for future tax seasons. This means considering how your business decisions today will impact your tax obligations in the years to come. For example, if you anticipate a significant increase in revenue next year, it may be beneficial to accelerate expenses or delay income to manage your tax bracket. Similarly, if you're planning to expand your business or make major investments, understanding the tax implications of those decisions now can help you prepare and avoid surprises later.

Finally, don't underestimate the value of professional assistance during tax season. Working with a qualified tax advisor or accountant can save you time, reduce stress, and ensure that you're taking full advantage of all available tax benefits. A professional can help you navigate complex tax laws, avoid common pitfalls, and provide peace of mind that your taxes are filed accurately and on time. They can also represent you in the event of an audit and provide guidance on tax planning strategies tailored to your business's unique needs.

In conclusion, preparing for tax season requires careful planning, organization, and attention to detail. By staying on top of your financial records, understanding your tax obligations, and seeking professional advice when needed, you can make tax season a more manageable and even beneficial time for your business. Effective preparation not only helps you meet your tax responsibilities but also positions your business for continued financial health and success.

Maximizing Your Deductions

Maximizing your deductions is one of the most effective ways to reduce your taxable income and keep more of your hard-earned money in your business. As a woman entrepreneur, understanding the full range of deductions available to you is crucial for minimizing your tax liability and enhancing your business's financial health. By strategically tracking and claiming all eligible expenses, you can significantly lower your tax bill and reinvest those savings back into your business.

To maximize your deductions, it's essential to keep thorough and accurate records of all business-related expenses throughout the year. Common deductions include everyday operational costs such as rent, utilities, office supplies, and insurance premiums. However, there are many other deductions that business owners often overlook, such as:

- **Home Office Deduction:** If you run your business from home, you may be eligible to deduct a portion of your home expenses, including mortgage interest, rent, utilities, and maintenance, based on the percentage of your home used exclusively for business purposes.

- **Vehicle Expenses:** If you use your vehicle for business purposes, you can deduct either the actual expenses incurred, such as gas, maintenance, and insurance, or use the standard mileage rate set by the IRS. Keeping a detailed log of your business mileage is essential for claiming this deduction.

- **Travel and Meals:** Business travel expenses, including airfare, lodging, and meals, are deductible if the primary purpose of the trip is business-related. Be sure to document the business purpose of the trip and retain receipts for all expenses. Meals are typically deductible at 50%, but in certain cases, such as during travel, they may qualify for a higher deduction.

- **Employee Benefits:** Contributions to employee health insurance plans, retirement plans, and other benefits are generally deductible. These deductions not only reduce your tax liability but also help you attract and retain top talent.

- **Depreciation:** The cost of business assets, such as equipment, machinery, and vehicles, can be deducted over time through depreciation. The IRS allows various methods for calculating depreciation, including the Section 179 deduction, which permits businesses to deduct the full cost of certain assets in the year they are purchased.

- **Continuing Education:** If you invest in your professional development or that of your employees through courses, workshops, or certifications, these expenses can often be deducted as business expenses.

Timing is also an important factor in maximizing your deductions. For example, if you anticipate being in a higher tax bracket next year, you might accelerate certain expenses into the current year to take advantage of the deductions when they can have the greatest impact. Conversely, if you expect your income to decrease, deferring deductions to the following year may be beneficial.

To ensure you're taking full advantage of all available deductions, consider working with a tax professional who understands the nuances of business taxation. A knowledgeable tax advisor can help you identify deductions you may not be aware of, ensure that you comply with IRS regulations, and develop a tax strategy that aligns with your business goals.

In conclusion, maximizing your deductions is a powerful way to reduce your tax burden and improve your business's bottom line. By staying organized, keeping detailed records, and being strategic about the timing of your expenses, you can make the most of the deductions available to you and keep more money in your business where it belongs.

CHAPTER 13

Retirement Planning

Retirement planning is a crucial aspect of financial management that often gets overlooked in the busy lives of entrepreneurs. As a woman entrepreneur, planning for your retirement is not just about ensuring a comfortable life after you step away from your business—it's also about making strategic decisions now that can lead to long-term financial security and peace of mind. By taking a proactive approach to retirement planning, you can create a financial cushion that supports your future while also offering potential tax benefits today.

Unlike employees of larger companies who may have access to employer-sponsored retirement plans, entrepreneurs must take the initiative to set up and contribute to their own retirement accounts. Several retirement plan options are available, each with its own benefits and considerations. One popular choice for small business owners is the Simplified Employee Pension (SEP) IRA, which allows you to contribute a percentage of your income, up to a certain limit, and offers the advantage of tax-deferred growth. Another option is the Solo 401(k), which is designed for self-employed individuals and provides higher contribution limits, allowing you to maximize your retirement savings.

In addition to traditional retirement accounts, consider the benefits of a Roth IRA. While contributions to a Roth IRA are made with after-tax dollars, the account grows tax-free, and qualified withdrawals in retirement are also tax-free. This can be particularly advantageous if you anticipate being in a higher tax bracket during retirement.

Retirement planning is not just about choosing the right account; it's also about making consistent contributions and managing your investments wisely. Start by setting clear retirement goals—consider when you want to retire, the lifestyle you envision, and the income you'll need to sustain it. Use these goals to determine how much you need to save each year and what investment strategies will help you reach your targets. Regularly review your retirement plan and adjust your contributions or investment choices as needed to stay on track.

Beyond the financial aspects, retirement planning also involves preparing for the transition out of your business. If you plan to sell your business or pass it on to a successor, it's essential to start planning well in advance. Consider how the sale or transfer will impact your retirement income and what steps you need to take to ensure a smooth transition. This might include grooming a successor, formalizing your succession plan, or working with a financial advisor to maximize the value of your business.

Finally, be sure to account for healthcare costs in retirement, which can be substantial. Planning for these expenses now, whether through long-term care insurance or other financial products, can protect your savings and provide peace of mind as you approach retirement.

Taking control of your retirement planning today ensures that when the time comes, you can step away from your business with confidence, knowing that you have a secure financial foundation in place.

Understanding Retirement Accounts

Choosing the right retirement accounts is a crucial step in securing your financial future as an entrepreneur. With a variety of options available, each offering different benefits and tax implications, it's important to understand how these accounts work, and which ones align best with your retirement goals.

The Simplified Employee Pension (SEP) IRA is a popular choice for small business owners due to its flexibility and high contribution limits. With a SEP IRA, you can contribute up to 25% of your net earnings from self-employment, up to a certain limit, making it an excellent option for those who want to save aggressively. Contributions to a SEP IRA are tax-deductible, reducing your taxable income for the year, and the investments grow tax-deferred until you withdraw the funds in retirement.

Another powerful tool for entrepreneurs is the Solo 401(k), designed specifically for self-employed individuals or small business owners with no employees, other than a spouse. The Solo 401(k) allows for both employee and employer contributions, which means you can contribute as both, maximizing your retirement savings potential. The combined contribution limit for a Solo 401(k) is significantly higher than many other retirement plans, and like the SEP IRA, contributions are tax-deductible, with tax-deferred growth.

For those looking to diversify their tax strategy, a Roth IRA offers a different set of advantages. Contributions to a Roth IRA are made with after-tax dollars, so while you don't get an immediate tax deduction, your investments grow tax-free, and qualified withdrawals in retirement are also tax-free. This can be particularly advantageous if you expect to be in a higher tax bracket in retirement, as you won't owe taxes on your withdrawals.

Each of these retirement accounts has specific rules regarding contribution limits, withdrawal penalties, and eligibility requirements. For example, Roth IRAs have income limits that may affect your ability to contribute directly, though there are strategies like the "backdoor" Roth IRA that can help high-income earners take advantage of this option. It's also important to note that required minimum distributions (RMDs) apply to SEP IRAs and Solo 401(k)s once you reach a certain age, while Roth IRAs do not have RMDs during the account holder's lifetime, offering more flexibility in your retirement planning.

Understanding these different retirement accounts allows you to make informed decisions about where to allocate your savings. Depending on your financial situation, you might benefit from using a combination of these accounts to balance tax advantages and maximize your retirement income. Consulting with a financial advisor can help you navigate these options and develop a retirement plan that aligns with your long-term goals.

By carefully selecting and managing your retirement accounts, you can build a robust financial foundation that supports a secure and comfortable retirement, allowing you to focus on your entrepreneurial journey with confidence.

Planning for Financial Independence

Achieving financial independence is a central goal for many entrepreneurs, representing the freedom to make choices without being constrained by financial necessity. For women entrepreneurs, planning for financial independence involves more than just accumulating wealth—it's about creating a sustainable financial strategy that supports your lifestyle, future goals, and personal values. To reach this milestone, you need to take a proactive and disciplined approach to managing your finances, both in your business and personal life.

The foundation of financial independence lies in building multiple streams of income, which can provide security and flexibility. This might include diversifying your business ventures, investing in income-generating assets like real estate or dividend-paying stocks, and creating passive income streams that continue to grow even when you're not actively working. By diversifying your income sources, you reduce your reliance on any single stream and increase your financial resilience against market fluctuations or economic downturns.

Equally important is controlling your expenses and living within your means, which allows you to save and invest more of your income. This doesn't mean depriving yourself but rather making intentional choices about how you spend your money, aligning your spending with your values and long-term goals. Establishing a solid budget and regularly reviewing your financial situation can help you identify areas where you can cut unnecessary costs and redirect those funds toward building wealth.

Investing strategically is another key element in planning for financial independence. This involves not only selecting the right investment vehicles but also understanding your risk tolerance and time horizon. A well-diversified investment portfolio that balances growth with stability can help you achieve your financial goals while managing risk. Regularly contributing to retirement accounts, such as a SEP IRA or Solo 401(k), ensures that you're consistently building wealth for the future, while also taking advantage of tax benefits.

As you move closer to financial independence, it's essential to plan for the long term by considering factors like inflation, healthcare costs, and changes in your financial needs over time. Creating a financial plan that includes a mix of short-term and long-term goals can help you stay on track and adjust your strategy as needed. It's also important to consider estate planning to ensure that your wealth is preserved and passed on according to your wishes.

Achieving financial independence doesn't happen overnight; it's the result of consistent effort, informed decision-making, and a commitment to your financial goals. By taking control of your financial future, you empower yourself to make choices that align with your vision for your life and your business. Whether you aspire to retire early, travel the world, or simply enjoy the peace of mind that comes with financial security, planning for financial independence is a journey that begins with thoughtful planning and disciplined execution.

CHAPTER 14

Succession Planning

Succession planning is a critical yet often overlooked aspect of business management, particularly for entrepreneurs who have built their companies from the ground up. As a woman entrepreneur, ensuring the continuity of your business beyond your active involvement is essential not only for preserving your legacy but also for securing the future of your employees, clients, and stakeholders. Succession planning involves preparing for the eventual transition of leadership, whether due to retirement, sale, or unexpected circumstances, and it requires careful consideration of both the financial and personal aspects of the process.

The first step in succession planning is identifying potential successors who can carry on the vision and values that have made your business successful. This could be a family member, a trusted employee, or an external candidate with the necessary skills and experience. Choosing the right successor is crucial, as they will be responsible for leading the company through its next phase of growth. It's important to assess not only their qualifications but also their commitment to the business's long-term goals and their ability to inspire and lead others.

Once a successor is identified, it's essential to develop a comprehensive plan for their transition into leadership. This process should include training and mentorship to ensure they are fully prepared to take on the responsibilities of running the business. Gradually increasing their involvement in decision-making and strategic planning can help them gain the confidence and experience needed to lead effectively. Additionally, it's important to establish clear communication with your team and stakeholders about the transition to maintain stability and trust during the process.

Financial considerations are also a key component of succession planning. This includes determining how the transfer of ownership will be handled, whether through a sale, transfer of shares, or other mechanisms. If you plan to sell the business, it's important to have a clear understanding of its value and to structure the sale in a way that maximizes your financial return while ensuring the continued success of the company. If you intend to pass the business on to a family member, careful estate planning is necessary to manage tax implications and ensure a smooth transfer of ownership.

Succession planning also involves preparing for unexpected events, such as illness or sudden departure. Having a contingency plan in place ensures that the business can continue to operate smoothly even in your absence. This might include designating an interim leader or establishing a decision-making protocol to guide the business during the transition.

Ultimately, succession planning is about securing the future of your business and ensuring that it continues to thrive under new leadership. By taking the time to carefully plan for this transition, you can leave a legacy and provide peace of mind for yourself, your family, and your employees. A well-executed succession plan not only protects the business you've worked so hard to build but also sets the stage for continued success in the years to come.

Preparing Your Business for Transition

Preparing your business for transition is a vital step in ensuring a smooth handover of leadership and ownership, whether you're planning to sell, retire, or pass the business on to a successor. This process involves more than just identifying a new leader; it requires making sure that your business is structurally, financially, and operationally ready for change. By taking deliberate steps to prepare your business, you can protect its value, maintain its stability, and facilitate a successful transition that aligns with your long-term goals.

One of the key aspects of preparing for a transition is ensuring that your business operations are well-documented and efficient. This includes having clear, written processes and procedures for all major functions, from daily operations to strategic decision-making. Documenting these processes not only helps the incoming leadership understand how the business runs but also ensures consistency and continuity during the transition period. Additionally, reviewing and streamlining operations can improve efficiency, making your business more attractive to potential buyers or successors.

Financial readiness is another critical factor in a successful transition. This involves ensuring that your financial records are accurate, up-to-date, and transparent. Potential buyers or successors will want to see a clear picture of the business's financial health, including profit margins, cash flow, and liabilities. Conducting a thorough financial audit before the transition can help identify any issues that need to be addressed and provide reassurance to those taking over. It's also important to have a solid understanding of the business's valuation, which will guide negotiations and help set realistic expectations for both parties.

Strengthening your business's customer and vendor relationships is also crucial in preparing for a transition. These relationships are often the backbone of a business, and their continuity can be a deciding factor in the success of the transition. Ensure that contracts with key customers and vendors are secure and clearly outlined and consider communicating the upcoming transition to these stakeholders in a way that reassures them of the business's ongoing stability and commitment to their needs.

Additionally, it's important to consider the impact of the transition on your employees. They are the ones who will continue to drive the business forward, so keeping them informed and engaged throughout the process is essential. Developing a plan for retaining key employees and providing them with support during the transition can help maintain morale and ensure that the business continues to operate smoothly. Offering incentives, such as bonuses or stock options, can also help retain talent and align their interests with the long-term success of the business.

Finally, preparing your business for transition includes setting a clear timeline and communicating it effectively to all involved parties. This timeline should outline key milestones and deadlines, helping to manage expectations and ensure that the transition progresses smoothly. By being transparent and proactive in your communication, you can build trust and minimize disruptions during the handover process.

In preparing your business for transition, you not only safeguard its legacy but also pave the way for continued success under new leadership. By focusing on operational efficiency, financial transparency, and strong stakeholder relationships, you can ensure that your business remains resilient and poised for growth long after you've stepped down.

Estate Planning Basics

Estate planning is a crucial component of managing your wealth and ensuring that your business and personal assets are distributed according to your wishes after your passing. For women entrepreneurs, estate planning is not only about safeguarding your family's financial future but also about preserving the legacy of your business. A well-crafted estate plan provides clarity, reduces the potential for disputes, and minimizes tax liabilities, all while ensuring that your business continues to thrive under new ownership or management.

At the heart of any estate plan is a comprehensive will, which outlines how your assets, including your business, should be distributed. Your will should clearly specify who will inherit your business, whether it's family members, business partners, or an external buyer. It's also important to appoint a trusted executor who will be responsible for carrying out your wishes and managing the legal and financial aspects of your estate. If your business is a significant part of your estate, you may also want to include specific instructions for its management or sale.

In addition to a will, many entrepreneurs benefit from establishing a living trust, which can offer greater control and flexibility in managing your assets during your lifetime and after your death. A living trust allows you to transfer ownership of your assets into the trust, which can then be managed according to your instructions. This can help avoid probate, the legal process of settling an estate, which can be time-consuming, costly, and public. A living trust also allows for a smoother transition of business ownership, as it can provide for the immediate transfer of control to a successor trustee upon your incapacity or death.

Another key element of estate planning is considering the tax implications of transferring your business and other assets. Estate taxes can significantly impact the value of the inheritance you leave behind, so it's essential to work with a financial advisor or estate planning attorney to develop strategies that minimize tax liabilities. This might include gifting shares of your business during your lifetime, setting up charitable trusts, or taking advantage of exemptions and deductions available under current tax laws.

It's also important to address contingencies, such as what happens if you become incapacitated and unable to manage your affairs. Establishing powers of attorney for both financial and healthcare decisions ensures that someone you trust is empowered to make decisions on your behalf if needed. This not only protects your interests but also provides clear guidance to your family and business associates during difficult times.

Regularly reviewing and updating your estate plan is essential to ensure that it reflects any changes in your personal or business circumstances, as well as changes in tax laws. Life events such as marriage, divorce, the birth of a child, or significant changes in your business can all necessitate revisions to your plan. By keeping your estate plan current, you can be confident that your wishes will be honored and that your legacy will be preserved.

In summary, estate planning is about more than just distributing your assets—it's about protecting your family, your business, and your legacy. By taking a thoughtful and proactive approach to estate planning, you can ensure that your business continues to prosper and that your loved ones are provided for according to your intentions.

CHAPTER 15

Part V: Personal Growth and Financial Leadership

Developing a Financially Savvy Mindset

Developing a financially savvy mindset is essential for any entrepreneur aiming to build a successful and sustainable business. As a woman entrepreneur, cultivating this mindset means not only mastering the technical aspects of financial management but also embracing a proactive, informed, and strategic approach to every financial decision you make. A financially savvy mindset empowers you to navigate challenges, seize opportunities, and make choices that enhance the long-term viability of your business.

At the core of a financially savvy mindset is the understanding that your financial health is integral to your business's overall success. This means consistently monitoring your finances, from cash flow and expenses to investments and liabilities, and using this data to make informed decisions. It's about always being aware of your financial position, so you can act quickly if adjustments are needed, whether that's cutting costs, scaling up, or exploring new revenue streams.

Another key element is recognizing the importance of continuous learning. The financial landscape is constantly evolving, with new tools, technologies, and strategies emerging that can impact how you manage your business. Staying informed about these developments, whether through reading, attending workshops, or seeking advice from financial professionals, ensures that you're always equipped with the knowledge to make the best decisions for your business. This mindset also involves being open to learning from your financial mistakes, viewing them as opportunities for growth rather than setbacks.

A financially savvy mindset also embraces strategic risk-taking. While it's important to manage risks carefully, successful entrepreneurs understand that calculated risks are often necessary for growth. This involves analyzing potential investments, understanding the risks involved, and being willing to act when the potential rewards align with your business goals. It's about balancing caution with the confidence to invest in your business's future, whether that's through expanding operations, entering new markets, or adopting innovative technologies.

Budgeting and financial planning are also central to developing this mindset. A financially savvy entrepreneur views budgeting not as a restrictive practice but as a strategic tool that helps guide decision-making. By setting realistic financial goals and creating detailed plans to achieve them, you can ensure that your business stays on track and remains financially healthy. This forward-thinking approach allows you to allocate resources effectively, anticipate challenges, and position your business for long-term success.

Finally, developing a financially savvy mindset means understanding the value of building and maintaining a strong financial support network. This includes accountants, financial advisors, mentors, and peers who can provide guidance, support, and insights as you navigate the financial complexities of entrepreneurship. Leveraging the expertise of others not only enhances your financial decision-making but also helps you avoid common pitfalls and seize new opportunities.

Incorporating these elements into your daily business practices will help you develop the financial acumen needed to make sound decisions, manage risks, and drive your business toward sustained growth and success. A financially savvy mindset is not just about managing money; it's about mastering the mindset that enables you to lead your business with confidence and clarity.

Overcoming Financial Fears

Financial fears are a common hurdle for many entrepreneurs, especially for women who may face unique challenges and societal pressures in the business world. These fears can stem from a variety of sources, such as the fear of making mistakes, the uncertainty of financial markets, or the pressure of managing cash flow and debt. While these concerns are natural, overcoming financial fears is essential for building confidence, making informed decisions, and driving your business forward.

The first step in overcoming financial fears is acknowledging them. It's important to recognize the specific fears that may be holding you back, whether it's the fear of not having enough capital, the fear of investing in growth, or the fear of financial instability. By identifying these fears, you can begin to address them head-on, rather than allowing them to influence your decisions subconsciously.

Education is a powerful tool in dispelling financial fears. Often, fear arises from the unknown or from a lack of understanding. By educating yourself on financial management, whether through courses, reading, or seeking advice from financial professionals, you can gain the knowledge and skills needed to navigate complex financial situations with confidence. The more you understand your finances, the less intimidating they become, allowing you to make decisions based on facts rather than fear.

Another effective strategy for overcoming financial fears is to break down large financial goals into smaller, manageable steps. For instance, instead of being overwhelmed by the idea of saving a large sum of money for a business expansion, focus on setting and achieving smaller milestones that gradually lead to your goal. This approach not only makes your financial goals more attainable but also builds your confidence as you see progress over time.

It's also important to reframe your mindset around financial risk. Rather than viewing risk as something to be feared, consider it an inherent part of entrepreneurship that, when managed wisely, can lead to significant rewards. Understanding that some level of risk is necessary for growth can help you move past the fear of failure and take calculated risks that are aligned with your business's long-term objectives.

Finally, seeking support from mentors, peers, or financial advisors can be invaluable in overcoming financial fears. These individuals can provide guidance, share their own experiences, and offer reassurance during challenging times. Having a support network helps you realize that you're not alone in facing financial fears and that many successful entrepreneurs have navigated similar challenges.

Overcoming financial fears is not about eliminating them entirely but rather about learning to manage them effectively so they don't hinder your progress. By educating yourself, breaking down goals, reframing risk, and seeking support, you can transform financial fear into financial empowerment. This shift in mindset will enable you to make confident, informed decisions that drive your business toward greater success.

Building Confidence in Financial Decision Making

Building confidence in financial decision-making is a transformative step for any entrepreneur, particularly for women who may face additional societal and internal pressures. Confidence in this area allows you to navigate the financial aspects of your business with clarity and assertiveness, making choices that are both strategic and aligned with your long-term goals. Developing this confidence is not just about mastering numbers; it's about trusting your judgment, understanding the financial landscape, and embracing the learning process that comes with every decision.

One of the foundational elements of building financial confidence is gaining a strong grasp of your business's financial health. This means regularly reviewing financial statements, understanding key metrics like cash flow, profit margins, and debt levels, and knowing how these factors influence your business's overall performance. The more familiar you are with your financial data, the easier it becomes to make informed decisions, whether you're considering an investment, budgeting for the future, or managing day-to-day expenses.

Experience also plays a crucial role in building confidence. Every financial decision, whether successful or not, provides valuable lessons that contribute to your growth as an entrepreneur. Embrace the outcomes of your decisions as learning opportunities, and over time, you'll develop a more intuitive understanding of what works best for your business. Remember, confidence often comes from action—making decisions, reflecting on the results, and using that knowledge to inform future choices.

Seeking input from financial professionals can further bolster your confidence. Collaborating with accountants, financial advisors, or mentors gives you access to expertise and perspectives that can validate your thinking or offer new insights. These relationships provide a sounding board for your ideas, helping you feel more secure in your decisions. However, it's important to balance this advice with your own judgment, ensuring that the final decision aligns with your vision for the business.

Another key to building confidence is setting clear financial goals. When you have a clear understanding of what you're working toward, it's easier to evaluate whether a decision moves you closer to or further from those goals. This clarity helps to eliminate doubt and uncertainty, allowing you to make decisions with greater conviction. Additionally, breaking down larger goals into smaller, achievable steps can give you the confidence boost that comes with each small victory.

Finally, cultivating a mindset that embraces risk as a natural part of entrepreneurship is essential. Understanding that not all financial decisions will be perfect—and that some level of risk is necessary for growth—helps you make decisions with confidence, even in the face of uncertainty. By accepting that mistakes are part of the process, you free yourself from the fear of failure, allowing you to take bold, calculated steps toward your business's success.

Building confidence in financial decision-making is a journey that evolves with experience, knowledge, and the willingness to learn. As you continue to make decisions, reflect on outcomes, and seek guidance when needed, your confidence will grow, empowering you to lead your business with assurance and clarity.

CHAPTER 16

Financial Negotiation Skills

Mastering financial negotiation skills is an invaluable asset for any woman entrepreneur. Whether you're negotiating with vendors, clients, investors, or even within your team, the ability to navigate financial discussions with confidence and precision can significantly impact your business's success. Strong negotiation skills enable you to secure better deals, protect your interests, and build mutually beneficial relationships that contribute to long-term growth.

The foundation of effective financial negotiation lies in thorough preparation. Before entering any negotiation, it's crucial to have a clear understanding of your objectives, the value of what you're negotiating, and the financial implications for your business. This involves doing your homework—researching market rates, understanding the other party's position, and identifying your walk-away point. By being well-prepared, you position yourself to negotiate from a place of strength, with a clear sense of what you're willing to accept and where you can be flexible.

Another key aspect of negotiation is the ability to communicate clearly and assertively. Confidence in your value and the terms you're proposing can greatly influence the outcome of the negotiation. It's important to articulate your needs and expectations while also actively listening to the other party's concerns and objectives. A successful negotiation often involves finding common ground where both parties feel they've gained something valuable. By fostering open, respectful communication, you can build trust and rapport, which are essential for reaching a favorable agreement.

Understanding the dynamics of leverage is also critical in financial negotiations. Leverage refers to the power you hold in the negotiation, which can come from various factors such as the uniqueness of your offer, your readiness to walk away, or the urgency of the other party's needs. Identifying and utilizing your leverage points can help you drive the negotiation toward a more favorable outcome. However, it's equally important to recognize when the other party has leverage and to adjust your strategy, accordingly, finding creative solutions that satisfy both sides.

Flexibility and creativity are often what set successful negotiators apart. While it's important to know your goals, being rigid in your approach can limit opportunities. Consider exploring alternative solutions or compromises that may offer unexpected benefits. For example, if a client is unable to meet your price point, you might negotiate for additional value in other areas, such as longer contract terms, upfront payments, or favorable payment schedules. Being open to different possibilities allows you to craft deals that work well for all parties involved.

Finally, practice is essential in honing your negotiation skills. The more you engage in financial negotiations, the more comfortable and adept you'll become at handling various scenarios. Reflect on each negotiation experience, analyzing what worked well and where improvements could be made. Over time, this continuous improvement will build your confidence and effectiveness as a negotiator, empowering you to secure deals that enhance your business's financial position.

Incorporating these strategies into your negotiation approach will not only help you achieve better financial outcomes but also strengthen your overall leadership as an entrepreneur. By mastering financial negotiation skills, you can ensure that your business thrives in even the most challenging and competitive environments.

Mastering Negotiation Techniques

Mastering negotiation techniques is a vital skill for women entrepreneurs looking to achieve favorable outcomes in business dealings. Whether you're negotiating a contract, securing investment, or discussing terms with a vendor, the ability to negotiate effectively can significantly enhance your business's success. Negotiation is both an art and a science—it requires understanding the dynamics of the conversation, employing strategic tactics, and adapting your approach based on the situation at hand.

One of the most fundamental techniques in negotiation is the ability to establish a strong opening position. Your opening offer sets the tone for the negotiation and anchors the discussion. It's important to start with a position that reflects your ideal outcome while leaving room for compromise. This technique, known as anchoring, can help you influence the direction of the negotiation and keep the conversation within a range that is favorable to you.

Another essential technique is to leverage the power of silence. After making a proposal or responding to an offer, allowing a moment of silence can be a powerful tool. It gives the other party time to consider your position and often compels them to fill the silence with further concessions or information. Silence can also be used to show that you are confident and in no rush to close the deal, which can shift the balance of power in your favor.

Building rapport and trust is also crucial in mastering negotiation. People are more likely to agree to terms when they feel a connection and trust the person they're negotiating with. Take the time to understand the other party's needs, concerns, and motivations. Showing empathy and finding common ground can lead to a more collaborative negotiation environment, where both parties work towards a mutually beneficial outcome.

In addition to these interpersonal techniques, it's essential to be adept at handling objections and counteroffers. When the other party raises objections or makes a counteroffer, it's important to listen carefully and respond thoughtfully. Rather than seeing objections as roadblocks, view them as opportunities to further understand the other party's priorities and to demonstrate the value of your offer. Reframing objections, asking clarifying questions, and providing additional information can help you overcome resistance and keep the negotiation moving forward.

Another advanced technique is the use of the "if-then" strategy. This involves framing your concessions or offers conditionally: "If you can meet this price, then I can extend the contract terms." This approach allows you to negotiate trade-offs that are advantageous to you while giving the other party something they value. The "if-then" technique is particularly effective because it creates a sense of reciprocity and encourages the other party to meet your needs in exchange for their own gains.

Finally, knowing when to walk away is a critical aspect of mastering negotiation. Not every deal is worth pursuing and understanding your walk-away point—the minimum acceptable terms—empowers you to negotiate without fear of losing the deal. If the negotiation reaches a point where the terms are no longer favorable or aligned with your goals, having the confidence to walk away can often lead to better opportunities down the line.

Mastering these negotiation techniques takes practice, but the payoff is substantial. By anchoring your position, using silence strategically, building rapport, handling objections, employing conditional offers, and knowing when to walk away, you can approach negotiations with greater confidence and skill. These techniques not only help you achieve better outcomes but also strengthen your ability to navigate complex business interactions with ease and professionalism.

Applying Negotiations to Financial Decisions

Applying negotiation skills to financial decisions is a powerful strategy that can significantly impact the success and sustainability of your business. Whether you're negotiating with lenders, investors, suppliers, or even customers, the ability to negotiate effectively can lead to better terms, lower costs, and increased profitability. Financial negotiations are not just about securing the best price—they're about creating value, managing risk, and aligning the terms of the deal with your business goals.

One of the most common financial negotiations entrepreneurs faces is with lenders and investors. When securing financing, whether through a bank loan or venture capital, the terms you negotiate can have long-lasting effects on your business's financial health. This includes negotiating interest rates, repayment schedules, equity stakes, and covenants. A successful negotiation in this context involves clearly understanding your business's financial needs and the cost of capital, as well as being able to articulate your business's value proposition and growth potential to justify favorable terms.

Supplier negotiations are another area where financial decisions play a crucial role. By negotiating better payment terms, discounts for bulk purchases, or more favorable delivery schedules, you can improve your cash flow and reduce operational costs. Effective supplier negotiations require a deep understanding of your cost structure and supply chain needs. It's also important to build strong relationships with your suppliers, as a collaborative approach often leads to more flexible and mutually beneficial agreements.

When it comes to pricing negotiations with customers, applying negotiation skills can help you achieve a balance between maximizing revenue and maintaining customer satisfaction. This might involve offering discounts for early payment, bundling services or products to add value, or negotiating long-term contracts that provide stable income streams. The key is to understand your pricing strategy and margins so that you can negotiate in a way that supports both your business's profitability and your customer's needs.

Negotiations can also be applied to managing overhead costs, such as leasing office space or purchasing equipment. Negotiating favorable lease terms, maintenance agreements, or extended warranties can reduce your fixed costs and provide greater financial flexibility. In these situations, being well-prepared with market research and a clear understanding of your budget constraints will give you the leverage needed to negotiate terms that align with your financial strategy.

Finally, applying negotiation techniques to employee compensation and benefits can help you attract and retain top talent while managing payroll costs effectively. Negotiating salary packages that include performance-based incentives, stock options, or flexible working arrangements can create a win-win situation where employees feel valued, and your business remains financially sound.

Incorporating negotiation into your financial decisions empowers you to make choices that enhance your business's financial stability and growth. By approaching these negotiations with confidence, preparation, and a clear understanding of your financial goals, you can secure terms that support your business's long-term success.

CHAPTER 17

The Future of Finance for Women Entrepreneurs

The future of finance for women entrepreneurs is poised to be transformative, as more women take the lead in shaping the global economy. As barriers continue to break down and access to resources expands, women are increasingly gaining the financial tools, knowledge, and networks necessary to thrive in business. This shift is not only empowering individual entrepreneurs but is also fostering greater diversity and innovation across industries. The rise of women-led businesses signals a future where finance is more inclusive, where women have equal opportunities to secure funding, scale their businesses, and influence financial markets.

Technology will play a significant role in this future, with fintech solutions making financial management, fundraising, and investment more accessible than ever before. Crowdfunding platforms, peer-to-peer lending, and blockchain technologies are opening new avenues for women to fund their ventures without relying solely on traditional banking systems, which have historically been more challenging for women to navigate. These technological advancements are leveling the playing field, allowing women entrepreneurs to connect directly with investors and customers who share their vision and values.

Moreover, the growing awareness and support for gender equality in finance are leading to the creation of more women-focused investment funds, grants, and mentorship programs. These initiatives are designed to address the unique challenges women face in accessing capital and provide them with the resources needed to succeed. As these programs continue to expand, they will help close the gender gap in business funding and encourage more women to pursue entrepreneurship.

However, the future also presents challenges that will require women entrepreneurs to be resilient and adaptable. Economic uncertainties, changing regulations, and evolving market demands will test the financial acumen and strategic thinking of business owners. To navigate these challenges successfully, women entrepreneurs will need to continue building their financial literacy, embracing lifelong learning, and staying ahead of industry trends.

In this evolving landscape, women entrepreneurs can redefine what success looks like in business and finance. By leveraging their unique perspectives, fostering inclusive business practices, and leading with purpose, they can drive meaningful change in the financial world. The future of finance for women entrepreneurs is bright, full of potential, and ripe for innovation—if women continue to push boundaries, seize opportunities, and support one another in their financial journeys.

Trends and Opportunities

As the business landscape evolves, several key trends and opportunities are emerging that women entrepreneurs can leverage to drive their success. One of the most significant trends is the rise of digital transformation, which is reshaping industries and creating new avenues for innovation. With the increasing accessibility of digital tools and platforms, women entrepreneurs have more opportunities to scale their businesses, reach global markets, and optimize operations. E-commerce, social media marketing, and data analytics are just a few examples of how technology is empowering women to build and grow businesses with greater efficiency and impact.

Another promising trend is the growing focus on sustainability and social responsibility in business. Consumers and investors alike are increasingly drawn to companies that prioritize ethical practices, environmental stewardship, and positive social impact. Women entrepreneurs, often driven by a desire to make a difference, are uniquely positioned to lead in this space. By aligning their business models with these values, they can tap into new markets, attract loyal customers, and access funding from socially conscious investors.

The shift towards remote work and flexible business models is also opening new opportunities for women entrepreneurs. The ability to run a business from anywhere allows for greater work-life balance and expands the talent pool, enabling women to build diverse, inclusive teams. This trend also reduces overhead costs and provides the flexibility to adapt quickly to changing market conditions.

In addition to these trends, there is a growing ecosystem of support for women entrepreneurs, including mentorship programs, networking groups, and women-focused venture capital funds. These resources provide valuable guidance, connections, and funding opportunities, helping women overcome traditional barriers and accelerate their business growth. As these networks continue to expand, they will play a crucial role in fostering a community of empowered women leaders who support and uplift one another.

Finally, the rise of financial technology (fintech) presents a wealth of opportunities for women entrepreneurs to access capital, manage finances, and streamline operations. From mobile banking to digital wallets and peer-to-peer lending platforms, fintech is democratizing finance and making it easier for women to start and grow their businesses. By staying informed about these technological advancements and integrating them into their business strategies, women entrepreneurs can enhance their financial management and unlock new avenues for growth.

The convergence of these trends presents a landscape rich with opportunities for women entrepreneurs. By staying agile, embracing innovation, and aligning their businesses with emerging trends, women can not only navigate the challenges of entrepreneurship but also seize the opportunities that will define the future of business.

Staying Ahead in the Financial Game

Staying ahead in the financial game is essential for women entrepreneurs who want to ensure long-term success and resilience in a competitive business environment. As the financial landscape continues to evolve, driven by technological advancements, market shifts, and regulatory changes, it's crucial to remain proactive and adaptable. This means continuously honing your financial acumen, staying informed about industry trends, and leveraging the latest tools and strategies to maintain a competitive edge.

One of the most effective ways to stay ahead is by embracing technology and integrating it into your financial management practices. Fintech innovations, such as artificial intelligence, blockchain, and data analytics, are transforming the way businesses operate and make decisions. By adopting these technologies, you can gain deeper insights into your financial performance, optimize your operations, and make data-driven decisions that enhance your business's profitability and growth.

Another key strategy is to cultivate a habit of lifelong learning. The financial world is dynamic, with new regulations, market conditions, and investment opportunities constantly emerging. To stay competitive, it's important to regularly update your knowledge through courses, workshops, and industry publications. Building a network of financial advisors, mentors, and peers can also provide valuable perspectives and advice, helping you navigate complex financial challenges and seize new opportunities.

Staying ahead also involves being proactive about risk management. This means regularly assessing your financial position, identifying potential risks, and implementing strategies to mitigate them. Whether it's diversifying your income streams, maintaining a strong cash reserve, or securing appropriate insurance, managing risk effectively ensures that your business can withstand economic uncertainties and continue to thrive.

In addition to these strategies, staying financially agile is crucial. The ability to adapt quickly to changing market conditions, pivot your business model, or explore new revenue streams can make all the difference in maintaining your competitive advantage. This agility requires a combination of strategic foresight, financial flexibility, and a willingness to innovate when necessary.

Finally, maintaining a forward-thinking mindset is essential for staying ahead in the financial game. This means not only focusing on immediate financial goals but also planning for the long-term future of your business. Whether it's preparing for expansion, succession planning, or investing in new markets, keeping an eye on the horizon ensures that you're always ready to capitalize on emerging opportunities.

By embracing these practices, women entrepreneurs can stay ahead in the financial game, ensuring that their businesses are not only competitive but also resilient and poised for continued success in an ever-changing landscape.

Conclusion: Empowering Your Financial Journey

As we bring this journey to a close, it's important to reflect on the incredible potential that lies within each woman entrepreneur. The financial strategies, insights, and skills discussed throughout this book are not just tools—they are keys to unlocking your fullest potential as a business leader. Mastering money management is more than just about balancing budgets and securing funding; it's about empowering yourself to make informed decisions, take calculated risks, and drive your business toward long-term success.

The path of entrepreneurship is filled with challenges, but it is also rich with opportunities. By cultivating a financially savvy mindset, embracing innovation, and continuously learning, you can navigate the complexities of the financial world with confidence and clarity. You are not just managing a business; you are shaping a future, one where women entrepreneurs play a pivotal role in the global economy.

Remember, financial success is not solely defined by the numbers on a balance sheet but by the impact you make, the legacy you create, and the lives you touch through your business. Whether you are just starting out or are well on your way in your entrepreneurial journey, the principles in this book are meant to guide you, inspire you, and equip you with the knowledge and confidence to achieve your goals.

As you move forward, continue to embrace the values of resilience, innovation, and purpose. Stay curious, stay bold, and never underestimate the power of your vision. The future of finance is bright, and as a woman entrepreneur, you can lead the way, setting new standards for success, equity, and empowerment.

Your journey doesn't end here—it's only just beginning. With the insights and strategies, you've gained, you are now equipped to take control of your financial destiny, build a thriving business, and inspire the next generation of women entrepreneurs. The world needs your leadership, your creativity, and your unwavering commitment to making a difference. The future is yours to shape—go out and create it.

© Copyright (2024) Catherine Ledger

All rights reserved